THE SEVEN WORDS FROM THE CROSS

A Commentary

Charles E. Wolfe

THE SEVEN WORDS FROM THE CROSS

ISBN 0-89536-420-4

PRINTED IN U.S.A.

CONTENTS

DEDICATION

For

Rev. Dr. George Wesley Buchanan

Rev. Dr. James T. Clemons

my teachers at

Wesley Theological Seminary

Washington D.C.

PREFACE

This commentary has emerged from the pastorate. It represents what I had wanted to know when I first started preaching the Seven Words more than twenty years ago. It is, therefore, offered to my colleagues in the pastorate. It is also offered to the laity who listen to us, hoping to hear the Word.

By setting each Word in its context, the commentary covers the entire period from placement upon the Cross until the death itself, as found in all four Gospels. The Greek text has been the basis of study, of course, but it has been written for the pastor and layperson with little or no Greek. Since the comparison of translations is the best way for the person who does not read Greek to gain insight into the range of possible meaning for the Greek words, six popular translations have been compared throughout: *King James Version* (KJV), *Phillips*, *Revised Standard Version* (RSV), *New English Bible* (NEB), *New American Bible* (NAB), and *Today's English Version* (TEV). As a convenience to the reader, TEV has been printed in full. It has been selected because it is the newest of the major translations.

Some translations have marginal readings. These represent either alternate translation possibilities, or else alternate readings based upon different manuscripts. These variant readings are mentioned wherever they have an interest or a bearing upon the interpretation of a text. In general, the manuscripts have not been identified by name or number because these designations would not be meaningful to the average reader.

Because of the development in ideas, of course, the Old Testament is fundamental for an understanding of the New Testament. In addition, I have made use of the non-canonical Jewish literature from roughly 200 B.C. to A.D. 100. In many cases, the "link" in idea between Old and New Testaments is found in this material. This literature is normally divided into two groups. That part of this material which Jerome included in the Latin Vulgate is called the *Apocrypha.* This is available to the English reader in both the King James Version, the Revised Standard Version, and the New English Bible. It includes the following books:

1 Esdras
2 Esdras
Tobit
Judith
Additions to Esther
The Wisdom of Solomon
Ecclesiasticus (or: Sirach)
Baruch
The Letter of Jeremiah
The Prayer of Azariah
Susanna
Bel and the Dragon
The Prayer of Manasseh
1 Maccabees
2 Maccabees

The remaining literature is generally called the *Pseudepigrapha.* The classic edition for the English reader is by R. H. Charles (Oxford: Clarendon Press 1913). It includes the following books:

Jubilees
The Letter of Aristeas
The Books of Adam and Eve
The Martyrdom of Isaiah
1 Enoch
The Testaments of the Twelve Patriarchs[1]
The Sibylline Oracles
The Assumption of Moses

---

[1]Normally cited by the name of the individual patriarch, e.g. *Testament of Levi.*

2 Enoch
2 Baruch
3 Baruch
4 Ezra
The Psalms of Solomon
4 Maccabees
Pirke Aboth
The Story of Ahikar
Fragments of a Zadokite Work

The average pastor would normally not have the time and resources to use this material, and so I have included references wherever they have helped my own understanding.

The Gospel of Peter is a non-canonical work which on occasion gives insight into the way in which the tradition developed. For the English reader, the relevant passages are given in foot-notes in *Gospel Parallels,* ed. by Burton H. Throckmorton, Jr. (New York: Thomas Nelson and Sons, 1949). The average pastor will probably not find enough of value to invest in a complete edition of the *Apocryphal New Testament.*

From time to time "the papyri" are mentioned. This is a general term for the mass of material which has been found to be of a non-literary nature. It includes shopping lists, receipts, wills, personal letters, contracts, and all of the other activities which are reduced to writing in the course of daily life. The inscriptions are usually grouped with the papyri. The value of this material is the evidence it provides for the way in which Greek words were used in every day life. Since the New Testament was written in a popular style, we can expect the same words to be used in the same way. Whenever usage in the papyri sheds light upon a word in the text, it has been mentioned for the additional insight it may provide for interpretation.

The commentary is based upon the text as we now have it. Higher critical questions are addressed only when they are unavoidable in interpreting the text. There is such a mass of material already available about the formation of the tradition itself that there is no need to add to it. Accordingly, no view of the Synoptic Problem is presupposed. The majority of New Testament scholars probably accept the hypothesis of the priority of Mark. In this view, texts from Mark are usually considered to be historically more valid than texts from other gospels. This is being challenged recently, however, so that it can no longer simply be taken for granted. If I have a view of the Synoptic Problem, it is the conviction that the solution is "unknowable." Therefore, in the commentary, each text is given equal weight.

This is a commentary on individual texts, although parallel accounts are considered. This means that it is not an attempted harmony. The problem with the harmony is that the initial presupposition forces the interpretation. My only conscious presupposition has been that these texts do represent the Word of God. It is our task to understand what they say, and not to be misled into looking for what we would like them to say.

The First Word

Luke 23:32-38

Verse 32.- *Two other men, both of them criminals, were also led out to be put to death with Jesus.*

The tradition is firm in all four gospels that two men were crucified with Jesus. In John 19:18, they are identified simply as "two others." In Luke, they are called "evil-doers" ("malefactors" in KJV and "criminals" in TEV). Outside of this section in Luke, the Greek word is found in the New Testament only in 2 Timothy 2:9, where Paul was chained like an "evil-doer" because he preached the gospel.

It is clear that the two men were not thieves in any normal sense of the word. Thieves break in and steal (Matthew 6:19) at unexpected times when all are asleep (Matthew 24:43), but they do not kill. This normal word for thief, from which "kleptomania" has come into English, is never applied to the two who were crucified with Jesus. The KJV translation of Mark 15:27 and Matthew 27:38 has given this mistaken impression. An entirely different word from "thief" is used in both places. Phillips, NEB, and TEV have "bandits" and RSV has "robbers." The thief works indoors, in secret without a weapon, but the robber works outdoors as part of a gang and violently attacks with weapons. This is the word used of the robber or bandit gang which attacked the Jew on the road to Jericho (Luke 10:30). Paul listed these robbers or bandits as one of the dangers which he endured on his missionary travels (2 Corinthians 11:26). The violence of the robber is suggested in Jesus' indignant remark to the crowd which had come to arrest him, "Do you have to come with swords and clubs to capture me, as though I were an outlaw?" (Matthew 26:55) It is possible, therefore, that the two men crucified with Jesus were violent outlaws, whose crimes against society included murder.

There is yet another possibility, however, for from the idea of the violence of the bandit, the word came to be used of the irregular guerilla soldier or rebel or terrorist. The word was applied to the Jews who continued active and violent resistance to Roman rule, and often seems to be synonymous with "zealot." It is in this sense that Barabbas is called a "robber" (John 18:40). The meaning is confirmed by the statement that Barabbas was involved in a bloody insurrection against Rome (Mark 15:7). Since Jesus was convicted by the Romans on a charge of treason, it is more probable that the three who were executed together were considered to be guilty of the same crime, than that two ordinary bandits were executed together with a political prisoner. The Latin versions also use the specialized word for a violent robber or guerilla soldier rather than the common word for thief or criminal. Even though Luke simply calls them "evil-doers," therefore, we should consider them as terrorists, rather than as simple thieves or even violent common criminals.

The Latin tradition has assigned names to the two men: Joathas or Zoathas and Maggatras or Chammatha. In addition, in some apocryphal accounts, the names are given as Titus and Dumachus or Dismas and Gestus.

"To be put to death" translates the Greek verb which means "to be raised up." From the idea of being raised up off the ground on a cross, the word came to mean "put to death," generally. Here, the full force of the original meaning is appropriate in reference to crucifixion.

Verse 33. *When they came to the place called "The Skull," they crucified Jesus there, and the two criminals, one on his right and the other on his left.*

Luke here uses the normal Greek word for "skull," which has come into English as "cranium." The Vulgate translation used the normal Latin word for skull, which has come into English as "Calvary." In Hebrew, it was called "Golgotha" (Matthew 27:33, Mark 15:22, and John 19:17). In the Old Testament, "golgotha" was used of a human skull (2 Kings 9:35) and also of a head count (Exodus 16:16, "let *each of you* take an omer"). In the New Testament, the word is found only in the accounts of the Crucifixion.

It is not known how or why the place came to be known as Golgotha. I have seen five different attempts at explanation: (1) An early Christian tradition affirmed that the cross had been placed directly over the buried skull of Adam. If the place had been called "Skull" because it was really believed that Adam had been buried there, however, it is simply inconceivable that it could have become a place of public execution. It would have been revered as a national shrine. This tradition was no doubt constructed from the idea that Jesus Christ is the second Adam. The proximity of the grave of Adam to the place of the death of Christ gives a perfect symbolism. Since the name is prior to the crucifixion, however, this tradition cannot be considered to have any historical validity. (2) Since it was a place of execution, it has been suggested that it was called "Skull" because the skulls of those who had been executed were left unburied on the site. This explanation would require the plural, "place of the skulls," and it is also unlikely that the Jews, with their attitude towards burial, would have allowed a pile of unburied skulls so close to the holy city. (3) It has been suggested that the name has nothing to do with the skulls of executed men, but rather that the contour of the area resembled a human skull and thus suggested the name. Our inability to locate this today is due to changes in the topography over the centuries which have so obliterated its appearance that the "skull" can no longer be seen. In the absence of any documentary evidence, there is nothing which can be said either in support of or in criticism of such a hypothesis. (4) Some have discovered a hill which, when seen from a certain angle, with a little imagination, appears to have the shape of a skull. This is today shown to tourists. (5) The explanation which requires the least hypothesizing assumes that the name had nothing to do with the shape or the appearance of the area. Since it was a place of execution, the skull was a nickname or symbol of the death which came to condemned men, much as a skull is placed upon a bottle of poison today. This is the most probable explanation.

Three different locations have been suggested, with varying degrees of acceptance by scholars. This is evidence that the exact site is not known. If one is not searching for a hill which looks like a skull, the most probable site appears to be the traditional one occupied by the Church of the Holy Sepulchre. The tradition is earlier than the fourth century, for the Emperor Constantine had reasons which seemed valid to him for the building of a memorial there to enclose the site of the Crucifixion and the empty tomb. Excavations have revealed that in the time of Jesus this was outside the city walls, where a place of execution would have to be. The immediate area had been used as a stone quarry, and tombs had been cut into the sides of the quarry. In A.D. 41 the new city wall was built to include this area.

Verse 34a. *Jesus said, "Forgive them, Father! They don't know what they are doing."*

About half of the oldest and best manuscripts include these words, and about half omit them. There are two possibilities: either (1) Luke wrote these words, and some of the scribes deliberately omitted; or (2) Luke did not write these words, and they were inserted by some of the scribes. The omission in many manuscripts can be accounted for on the basis of a wide-spread feeling that such a monstrous crime as the crucifixion simply could not be forgiven the Jews. The feeling which could produce persecution of the Jews even into modern times could easily lead to the omission of a few words. Since the Jews were so completely identified with the city of Jerusalem, the destruction of the holy city at the hands of the Romans seemed evidence to many people that they had in fact not been forgiven, and that the favor of God had been withdrawn from them and, especially from the time of Constantine, given to the Christians instead. It is even possible that they were considered genuine words of Jesus better left unsaid. For these reasons, even if Luke had written the words, they could well have been omitted in many manuscripts.

The other possibility is that Luke did not write these words, and, therefore, the manuscripts without them faithfully reproduce Luke. In this case, they were added by scribes. This does not mean that Jesus did not speak the words — for no one would dare to invent deliberately such a word unless there had been a reliable tradition that Jesus had actually spoken it. If indeed some of the scribes inserted the words from the oral tradition, this would make them genuine words of Jesus, but not a part of the original manuscript of Luke. This apparently happened also in Luke 6:5, where one manuscript inserted what I consider to be a genuine saying of Jesus from the oral tradition which Luke himself probably did not write: "On a Sabbath Jesus saw a man working and said to him, 'Man, if you know what you are doing you are blessed; but if you do not know, you are cursed and a a violator of the Law.' " The story of the woman taken in adultery seems to be another example. The fact that it is found in so many places in different gospels in the various manuscripts is evidence that it did not originally belong in any one particular place but was a free-floating part of the oral tradition. This does not mean that it is not genuine. There must have been many of these genuine sayings and stories which circulated in the oral tradition which did not become a part of any of the gospels. In the case of this text, the evidence is so evenly divided that it is not possible to be certain whether Luke wrote these words or not, but they have the ring of truth, and may be considered as authentic words of Jesus.

The basis upon which Jesus asks the Father to forgive them is their ignorance of the full implications of their actions. It is therefore assumed that, if they had truly recognized Jesus as the Son of God, they would not have dared to participate in the crucifixion, even indirectly. The forgiveness is inclusive. If the Romans had truly known, they would have refused to carry out the execution. If the crowds had known it, they would have stopped the crucifixion. If the Jewish leaders had known, they would have received the Messiah with joy. Because they did not know, however, they performed these acts.

It is noteworthy that Jesus does not offer the forgiveness himself, but asks the Father to grant it. This is a significant theology of the Cross in which the Father is as actively involved in the act of redemption as is the Son.

Since the forgiveness envisioned here is for sins committed without knowledge, repentance on the part of the sinner is not involved. In this word, therefore, we see the deepest and most basic meaning of the Cross — in a provision for wiping the slate clean and allowing each person to begin anew without the crippling load of guilt from the past. In this sense, it is an offer from the Cross which opens possibilities for the future which otherwise would have been closed. This is the idea of justification. This word, however, does not apply to subsequent sins committed deliberately or in knowledge of the consequences. For that, repentance must be considered.

This most basic forgiveness is uniquely Christ's and uniquely related to the Cross. It does provide, however, the necessary basis for the Christian life, and allows for the possible responses of love and faith to become normative. Because of the forgiveness clause in the Lord's Prayer, it is understood that each person who has experienced this basic offer of forgiveness from the Cross will then extend the forgiveness to others in our varied human relationships.

Verse 34B. *They divided his clothes among themselves by throwing dice.*

The task of performing a crucifixion was so distasteful that the custom arose of making it somewhat more palatable by assigning to the soldiers, as a bonus, the clothing and personal effects of the condemned man. John 19:23-24 gives the additional detail that there were four soldiers, and so they divided the clothing and personal effects into four piles of roughly equal value. It seemed a shame to destroy the seamless robe by cutting it into four parts, however, and so they decided to cast lots or throw the dice for it, winner take all. The lots or the dice used may have been stones, either of different colors or with designs upon them.

The Romans used the sacred lot to determine the will of the gods in much the same manner as the Jews. In Latin, however, there is reflected a change in attitude, for the word also came to be used as a means of deciding something by pure chance rather than by the will of the gods. That would appear to be the meaning here, and TEV catches the flavor with "throwing dice" rather than "casting lots," which would carry in English a stronger religious overtone than was intended. Lady Luck was a part of the Roman Pantheon, and so it could be said that, ultimately, there are sacred associations even in shooting dice. It yet seems evident that to these soldiers it had the same meaning that it has to a Las Vegas gambler who blows upon his dice and utters his own prayer to Lady Luck as he crouches at the crap table.

To the Gospel writers, however, the casting of the lot retained its sacred associations. John quotes Psalms 22:18, in which enemies gamble for the clothing with hostile intent. Paul shows the continuance of the sacred context in Ephesians 1:11, in the verbal form of the casting of lots, to indicate God's determination of destinies: "God chose us to be his own people." If we can assume that Luke would see the lot in the same way, there would be an air of bitter, even if unconscious, blasphemy in the picture of soldiers casting lots for the clothing of the Son of God. It would seem as if they had taken upon themselves the right to determine the destiny of God himself. This unconscious blasphemy is no doubt part of what is forgiven the soldiers.

In spite of the air of blasphemy, there is a sense in which it was necessary that this be done. In Philippians 2:6-8, Paul speaks of the complete humbling of Christ which had to occur before salvation would be possible. The appropriation of the clothing and personal effects of a living man is to treat him as if he were already dead. It cuts the last tie to this earth. All that now remains is to give up the last breath. The complete poverty of Jesus is graphically expressed, for even the poorest of the poor have at least their own rags. Through this complete and necessary impoverishment, Christians have been immeasurably enriched by means of union with Christ (1 Corinthians 1:5).

Verse 35. *The people stood there watching while the Jewish leaders made fun of him:*

"He saved others; let him save himself if he is the Messiah whom God has chosen!"

"The people stood there watching." The noun formed from the verb translated as "watching" is used in the papyri of seeing the sights as a tourist, of theatrical displays, and of village spectacles of various kinds. Public executions were popular shows in this vein, and the verb used carries the suggestion of watching an entertainment. Matthew 27:39 and Mark 15:29 affirm that the people joined in the mockery. It should be noted that in Psalms 22:7 the people mock the sufferer. John does not mention the mocking.

The word translated as "people" indicates the average common population as distinct from the aristocracy. This is the primary meaning here. The word also had a technical sense of the *people of God*, in distinction from the rest of the world. In the Greek Old Testament, it would refer to Israel, and in the rest of the New Testament to Christians. Romans 9:25 ties Israel and Christians together by quoting an Old Testament text. 1 Peter 2:9 clearly uses this word to indicate Christians as the holy people of God. This word has come into English as "laity." There well may be an overtone of irony that the people of God would mock the Son of God — an overtone that goes beyond the simple designation of the crowd in contrast to the rulers.

"While the Jewish leaders made fun of him." The translations vary between "rulers" (KJV, RSV, Phillips, and NEB) and "leaders" (TEV and NAB). The word is used of magistrates as government officials, of rulers of synagogues, and, loosely, of leading citizens. Once it is used of the president of an athletic club. The reference here is probably to the members of the Sanhedrin who had voted the condemnation of Jesus. They were the leading Jews, and they had some official position, both religiously and governmentally, under the Romans.

There is great variation in the translation of the verb: "derided" (KJV), "scoffed" (RSV), "continued to scold" (Phillips), "jeered" (NEB and NAB), and "made fun of" (TEV). The verb is built upon the word for "nose," and originally meant to make some sort of a movement with the nose against some one as a mark of contempt or ridicule. In Luke 16:14, it is used in the context of Jesus' teaching that one cannot serve both God and money. The Pharisees then made fun of the teaching. In Galatians 6:7, Paul uses this verb in the warning that God cannot be made a fool of, for a person will reap what he sows.

"He saved others; let him save himself." The primary meaning of the verb translated as "save" is rescue from death, calamity, disease, or demon possession. In the papyri are found "since, therefore, your life has been saved in sickness by the great god Socnopaeus" and "when I was in danger at sea he saved me." The Jewish leaders, no doubt, are recognizing the healing ministry of Jesus in the use of this word. Even if they admitted the healing miracles, however, they did not believe the gospel of the Miracle Worker. The assumption behind the words of mockery is that no one would remain upon a cross to die painfully if he had the power to prevent it. If Jesus remains upon the cross, therefore, it is because he cannot rescue himself from this death. This is evidence that Jesus is not the Messiah, for the powerful Messiah could not be held upon a cross. It would not occur to them that the Messiah would submit to a voluntary death as a means of providing an atonement between sinful humanity and God. The verb "save" has a second meaning which would not occur to the Jewish leaders in this context, but would probably be in the mind of the Christian reader, and would underscore the dreadful irony of the scene. To "save" also means to preserve from eternal death by giving eternal life. The "saving" which Jesus accomplished in this sense of the word is far more significant than the "saving" of a

few sick people from various diseases. It is only as Jesus refused to save himself in the physical sense that he became able to save others in the eternal sense.

"... *if he is the Messiah whom God has chosen!*" The translations have: "Messiah" (TEV and NAB), "Christ" (KJV, RSV, and Phillips), and "Anointed" (NEB). These are simply the Hebrew, Greek, and English equivalents, respectively. Even though anointing in the Old Testament was applied to prophets and priests as well, the primary anointing was of the king as a sign that he had been selected by God. The word "messiah" thus came to mean "king," and it has never lost this royal association. From the promise to David, that his seed would sit upon the throne forever (2 Samuel 7), the idea took root that this Messiah must be a son of David. As the earthly kings failed, and especially during the period of national disaster, the Messiah of the seed of David came to be seen as the Warrior King, who would destroy the enemies of God's people and restore to them forever the glories of the Davidic monarchy.

By the time of Jesus, the expectation of the Warrior King had focused upon the overthrow of the Roman oppressors. Because of the religious intensity of the feast and because Jerusalem served as a magnet to draw huge crowds, every Passover became a tinder box ready to flame into open revolt should the conviction develop that the Messiah had appeared to lead his people to victory against the enemies of God. Two examples of this expectation may be given from outside the Old Testament. The Eagle Vision of 4 Ezra 11-12, originally composed within the first century A.D., specifically applied this type of Messianic expectation to Rome as the last oppressor of the people of God. Since the eagle was the national emblem of Rome, the allusion is unmistakable. In 4 Ezra 12:31-34, the Lion of Judah appears to rebuke the Eagle for his crimes. This Lion of Judah is of the seed of David and therefore clearly the

Messiah. After rebuking the wicked Romans to their face, he will destroy them.

Also using material from the first century, 2 Baruch thinks of the Messiah as the Warrior King. In 2 Baruch 40:1-4, the last enemy king left alive will be captured by the Messiah and taken to Mount Zion, where he will first be convicted of his sins and then put to death. The rule of the Messiah will then continue forever, until the world of corruption is at an end. Jerusalem, the holy city, is to be the site of this eternal Messianic Kingdom.

These texts, no doubt, reflect accurately the reason why the people desired to make Jesus the Warrior King, and probably explain the Triumphal Entry into Jerusalem on Palm Sunday. They also explain the nervousness of Pilate in the face of a constant potential for explosion at Passover. To many, including the Jewish leaders, Jesus' choice of a different model for the Messiah was so inexplicable that they could only conclude that he was a blasphemous imposter. The Messiah could not have been placed upon a cross in the first place, but even if so, he could not be kept there. That Jesus remained upon the cross, therefore, was incontrovertible evidence in their eyes that he was *not* the Messiah.

"Whom God has chosen" translates a Greek word which could also be rendered "the Elect One." The translations uniformly give some form of "Chosen One." Normally, whatever is chosen is the best of its class, and therefore, the word may refer to the choicest cypress trees (2 Kings 19:23) and the picked fighting men of Israel (Psalms 78:31). From this general idea, the word came to be used specifically of the chosen people in covenant with God (Psalms 89:3). The "Elect One" usually meant Israel as a whole rather than an individual (Isaiah 42:1 and 45:4). The New Testament applies to Christians the title of "the chosen ones" (Matthew 24:31 and 1 Peter 2:9) in the sense of the people in covenant with God. The singular "Elect One" refers to the Messiah as an individual, rather than to a corporate whole, in the quotation of Isaiah 28:16 found in 1 Peter 2:6. In the Transfiguration story, Luke 9:35 refers to Christ as "the one having been chosen." Even though that is a participle rather than a verbal adjective as here, one manuscript there has the same form as here, the "Elect One." In John 1:34, in connection with the voice at the baptism of Jesus, some manuscripts have "the Elect of God" instead of "the Son of God." The Messiah is also called the Elect One in Enoch 40:5. Even if it is not a common title for the Messiah, therefore, there is yet a persistent minor tradition which is reflected in the words of the Jewish leaders.

Verse 36a. *The soldiers also made fun of him;*

The translations vary between "mocked" (KJV, RSV, Phillips, and NEB) and "made fun of" (NAB and TEV). This is a different Greek verb from that used to describe the mocking of the Jewish leaders. Jesus has predicted this mocking (Mark 10:34). In Luke 14:29, this verb is used of the ridicule heaped upon the man who was unable to complete the building of the tower. In Matthew 27:29, the soldiers ridicule Jesus by offering the crown of thorns and the purple robe and kneeling before the pretend king. In Luke 22:63, while holding Jesus for the appearance before the Sanhedrin, the soldiers mock the prophetic claim made for Jesus by blindfolding him, striking a blow, and then, in a mocking way, asking him which of them had delivered the blow.

The change of tense between the mocking of the Jewish leaders and that of the soldiers may be significant. The Jewish leaders repeatedly continued to mock Jesus (imperfect), while the soldiers simply mocked (aorist as equivalent to a simple past tense), perhaps indicating that they did it once and then tired of the "sport."

Verse 36b. ... *they came up to him and offered him cheap wine.*

The liquid is called "vinegar" (KJV and RSV), "sour wine" (NAB), and "cheap wine" (TEV). Vinegar is made by diluting alcoholic liquids such as cider and wine, and contains acetic acid. "Acetic" comes from the Latin word for "vinegar," and "vinegar" comes into English from two Latin words which mean "sour wine." The Greek word *(oxos)* occurs in the New Testament only in the texts relating to the crucifixion. This is not regular wine, for there was a different tax upon it than upon regular wine. A receipt from A.D. 357 is for a quantity of this liquid which was supplied by a vendor to soldiers stationed in Hermopolis. A contract from the sixth century exchanges this year's sour wine harvest for next year's sweet wine harvest. The Vulgate translated by "acetum," which is wine-vinegar. It is often identified with "posca," which was made from wine-vinegar, water, and egg. This was much cheaper than regular wine, and therefore popular with the soldiers and with the lower ranks of society. If this is the liquid intended, then "vinegar" does not give the idea to the English reader, for we simply do not use vinegar as an inexpensive drink. "Sour wine" is descriptive of the taste, but "cheap wine" gives the most accurate picture. In this particular context, the mockery consists in giving the cheap wine of the lower classes to one they called the king. In the later scene, however, in which the soldiers dipped a sponge in the same cheap wine and offered it to Jesus to ease his thirst, it is an act of kindness rather than an act of mockery, since they shared what they themselves had to drink.

The other possible interpretation sees an act of mockery in both cases. This is based upon considering the liquid to be "vinegar" rather than cheap wine. In the Septuagint, this word occurs regularly as a translation for the Hebrew word for vinegar *(chometz)*. This vinegar was usually made from grape wine which had gone sour or had been over-fermented. It was sometimes diluted and used as a drink, but primarily it was used as a table seasoning (Ruth 2:14). It was so acidic that it smarted when poured over a wound (Proverbs 25:20), and it hurt the teeth as smoke hurts the eyes (Proverbs 10:26). It tasted so bad that as a drink it can be compared with poison as a food (Psalms 69:21). If there is a reference here to Psalms 69:21 as a Messianic text which is fulfilled, then "vinegar" would be the preferred translation, and it would be a part of the humility. It seems more likely, however, that the common cheap wine of the lower classes is intended.

Verse 37. . . . *and said, "Save yourself if you are the King of the Jews!"*

This mockery of the soldiers has a double reference, echoing the taunt of the Jewish leaders and echoing the ironic sign placed over the cross.

Verse 38. *Above him were written these words: "This is the King of the Jews."*

Sometimes the name of the person to be executed and the crime of which he had been convicted were written on some sort of placard and placed around his neck. As he walked to the place of execution the crowd could readily identify him by name and by crime. Then the placard would be placed upon the cross itself. The text does not mention similar signs on the crosses of the two terrorists, and so we are probably to understand that a sign was placed only upon the cross of Jesus. In Matthew 27:37, it is specifically identified as the crime of Jesus, or the charge against him. Luke simply calls it the "epigraph" (the Vulgate has "superscription"). Mark 15:26 has the fuller text, saying that it was the epigraph of his crime. John 19:19-20 adds the information that it was in the three popular languages (Hebrew, Greek, and Latin), so that every passer-by would be able to read it in his own language. John calls it a "title" which could also mean the ground upon which an accusation could be made against some one.

Pilate was aware of the fact that Jesus had not claimed to be an earthly king, and therefore intended the sign as an ironic "dig" at the Jewish leaders, rather than as a straight-forward statement of charge and guilt of a condemned man. The picture of the King of the Jews on a cross is a reminder that the Jews are a subject race, and that anyone who would dare to claim kingship over such a people would end up on a cross like "this one." The Jewish leaders were annoyed by the sign, but could do nothing about it. On a deeper level, there is a dreadful irony in the sign, for the Christian conviction is that Christ is indeed the King of the Jews. The New Testament came to identify all Christian believers as the true Israel of the Old Testament. In spite of the mocking intent of Pilate, Christians see in the sign an involuntary tribute to the royalty of the Messiah.

The Second Word

Luke 23:39-43

Verse 39. *One of the criminals hanging there hurled insults at him: "Aren't you the Messiah? Save yourself and us!"*

In Matthew 27:44, both of the terrorists speak bitterly to Jesus, but here only one of them taunts Jesus. One possible explanation of the discrepancy is that they both began by taunting Jesus, but then the one began to sense that more was really happening here than appeared on the surface. He would first stop making insults himself and then begin to move towards faith. The other, who would never come to faith, continued the insult. This would assume that Matthew recorded the first stage in which both taunted Jesus, while Luke recorded only the second stage in which the second one has already begun his move towards faith. The other possible explanation of the discrepancy is that two different traditions are recorded in the two accounts. Matthew knew only that the terrorists on the cross had joined in the mockery, but Luke knew that one of them actually came to faith.

This terrorist had heard the taunt of the Jewish leaders: "if you are the Christ." By changing the cry to — "aren't you the Christ?" — he made the taunt even more bitter. Instead of making fun of a man pretending to be the Messiah ("if"), the terrorist made fun of an impotent Messiah ("you are").

Translations vary: "hurled insults" (TEV), "railed" (KJV and RSV), "covered with abuse" (Phillips), "taunted" (NEB), and "blasphemed" (NAB). The Greek word is "blasphemed," and the English word has come directly from it with the same spelling. The problem in translation, however, is that no single English word has the same range of meanings. The root idea is *speech which is motivated by evil* or *hostile intent against another.* When aimed at another human being, it is abuse or insult or mockery or slander (as in Mark 7:22 and Ephesians 4:31). Since the terrorist has not shown any belief that Jesus is more than a man, this would seem to be the intent of his language, and it is reflected in most of the translations. As a Jew, he would probably share in the common expectation of the Messiah as the Warrior King, and would intend his words to be taken as a mocking insult. The sense of the disparity between the painful death which would soon engulf all three of them and the Messianic pretensions of Jesus would add an extra viciousness to his words. When the slander is aimed at God, however, it is blasphemy (Matthew 9:3) in the technical sense which English has adopted for the word. Luke would intend the reader to understand that what the man intended only as a taunt against another man was in reality blasphemy. To apply the title "Christ" without believing in its truth, when it really is true, is blasphemy in the full religious sense of the word. The double meaning which the word would carry in this context cannot be reproduced in English.

Verse 40. *The other one, however, rebuked him saying, "Don't you fear God? You received the same sentence he did."*

"The other one, however, rebuked him, saying." The word translated as "rebuked" (KJV, RSV, NAB, and TEV) or "checked" (Phillips) or "answered sharply"

(NEB) has a deeper theological meaning than might be supposed on the surface. The Greek verb originally meant to evaluate some one or some thing, and then measure out the appropriate response. The response could be punishment or rebuke, but it could also be honor and praise. This particular form of the verb came to indicate a response of rebuking more often than a response of praise. In the Septuagint, the verb is used of the power of God as expressed towards the world. The pillars of heaven tremble at God's rebuke (Job 26:11). God has the power to "rebuke" creation by right of his being the Creator. The New Testament continued this association of the right to rebuke with divine Lordship. Accordingly, the storm ceased when Jesus "rebuked" the winds (Matthew 8:26), the fever left a sick woman under the "rebuke" of Jesus (Luke 4:39), and a demon was compelled to leave a boy it had possessed when it was "rebuked" by Jesus (Matthew 17:18). It is the right of the Son of God to issue a rebuke in an unqualified way as a superior to an inferior. It is very different when men and women rebuke each other, for then, since we are all sinners equally under the judgment of God, we can do this only when unconditional forgiveness will be granted to the one rebuked (Luke 17:3). Christians are not to rebuke each other lightly or spontaneously. They are first to pray about it, and then do it only in fear and trembling.

People have always arrogated to themselves the right to judge others, however, and to rebuke them as a superior to an inferior. When the people brought the children to Jesus, the disciples took it upon themselves to issue a rebuke. Jesus challenged their right to issue a rebuke, and offered to receive the children anyway (Mark 10:13-14). When the blind beggar cried out to Jesus for healing, the crowd rebuked him; but Jesus reversed their rebuke and healed the man anyway (Mark 10:48-49). The most dramatic instance is Peter's assumption of the right to rebuke Jesus for saying that the Son of Man must die. Jesus called this rebuke a temptation of Satan (Mark 8:32-33).

It is highly significant, therefore, that Jesus allowed the one man on the cross to rebuke the other. Jesus' silence concerning the rebuke itself, coupled with the promise of salvation in response to his petition, must be taken as approval of the rebuke. The rebuke is acceptable because it has come from a standpoint of penitence and not from an assumption of superiority to another.

"Don't you fear God?" Many times in the Bible the fear of God is natural response which righteous men and women make to the felt presence of the holiness and power of God. In this sense, *to have fear for God* represents a proper and positive attitude. It is a fear which is virtually awe and reverence, rather than terror. In this text, however, the fear of God seems to be the basic fear of the judgment of God after death and the likelihood of condemnation, rather than awe and reverence. As such, this is the lowest level of the fear of God, motivated largely by selfishness; yet it should be noted that even this is acceptable to Christ in his loving grace. The terrorist asks his companion if not even this elemental fear of judgment operates to restrain him from adding to the sum of the sins for which he must answer to God so soon. Can you be so coarse and callous as to taunt even a fellow sufferer? To say nothing of patient submission to the will of God, or any higher religious feeling, do you not even fear the judgment of God? The unspoken implication is that at a time like this a person should be preparing himself to meet God face to face. This is the proper object for thought, rather than continuing vicious and violent attitudes even at the very last moment of life.

"You received the same sentence he did." The word is variously translated as "condemnation" (KJV and RSV), "punishment" (Phillips), and "sentence" (NEB,

NAB, and TEV). Elsewhere in the New Testament the word is used of God's eternal punishment or sentence of condemnation against sinners and evil spirits. It is more likely, however, that the reference here is to the sentence of death pronounced against all three of them by the Roman government. Even if their crimes had been somewhat different, they had yet received the same sentence, but there may be an intention to suggest that they had all received the same sentence upon conviction of the same charge of treason.

Verse 41. *Ours, however, is only right, because we are getting what we deserve for what we did; but he has done no wrong.*

"Ours, however, is only right." Perhaps the sharp contrast between the insults heaped upon Jesus by the crowd and his fellow condemned sufferers on the one hand, and the prayer for forgiveness to be granted them made by Jesus on the cross, on the other hand, made an impression upon the one terrorist. No matter how he might once have felt about the crimes he had committed in his revolutionary cause, he now began to think about facing God. All of that was now behind him and he was as good as dead. He must have felt something in the man beside him which he had not felt in other men. Whatever it was, this had led him to confess that the punishment inflicted upon himself and his companion was fair. The translations vary: "justice" or "justly" (KJV, RSV, and NEB), "fair enough" (Phillips), "we deserve it" (NAB), and "right" (TEV). The Greek word is an adverb which expresses ideas of justice and right. A papyrus dated in 218 B.C. uses this adverb in a complaint that the division of a piece of property had not been made "fairly." In 1 Peter 2:23, this word is used of the fair judging of God. It is an easy transition from the idea of justice in a human court to divine justice. Since the word is commonly used

in both senses, greater point is given to the admission of the terrorist that his own punishment at the hands of his human judge is fair, and at the same time prepares the way for his asking Christ for an ultimate judgment which is merciful rather than fair.

"*. . . because we are getting what we deserve for what we did.*" "What we deserve" translates a single Greek adjective, which describes something which corresponds to or is of equal value with something else. Whatever corresponds to something else is worthy or comparable or suitable. Suffering in this world does not compare with the glory to come (Romans 8:18), but a worker is entitled to his food (Matthew 10:10) because there is a proper correspondence between labor and wages. Death is a suitable penalty for sin, and therefore the punishment on the cross is fitting for the crimes committed by the terrorists. Translators have expressed this by "what we deserve" (TEV and Phillips), "the due reward" (KJV and RSV), and "paying the price" (NEB and NAB).

"*. . . but he has done no wrong.*" Except for the KJV ("amiss"), translations agree upon "wrong." The Greek word is unusual, occurring only three times in the New Testament. From the basic meaning of "out of place," it came to indicate first, what is unfitting, unusual, or absurd, and then, unsuitable, improper, or morally wrong. In the papyri, it is used of malicious vandalism and of scandalous speech. Elsewhere, it is found in Acts 28:6 to indicate that no "wrong" or harm came to Paul when the snake bit him, and in 2 Thessalonians 3:2, where it is joined with a common word for "wicked" to describe certain men. The Latin tradition, together with one major Greek manuscript, has in this verse the same word for "wicked" which is used in Thessalonians. This represents an interpretation of its meaning rather than the genuine text. Like our English word "wrong," it can indicate a range of meaning all the way from the merely improper to the clearly criminal. Probably by the choice of this word, Luke represented the terrorist as meaning that Jesus has not even done anything questionable, let alone anything deserving of death.

Verse 42. *And he said to Jesus, "Remember me Jesus, when you come as King!"*

"And he said to Jesus, 'Remember me, Jesus.' " The better manuscripts have simply, "And he said, 'Jesus . . .' " TEV has inserted "to Jesus," without manuscript support, in the interests of clarity. KJV follows several Greek manuscripts and the Latin Vulgate: "And he said to Jesus, 'Lord . . .' " The "Lord" was added in order to magnify the man's confession of faith. This then required changing "Jesus" as the case of address to "to Jesus" as the indirect object of the speech. There is no question but that Luke wrote the simple "Jesus," and this may, in effect, heighten the idea of the salvation which is inherent in the word, "Jesus." There is generally such confusion over the names and titles applied to Jesus in the various manuscripts, however, that it is impossible to make much of a theological or homiletical point out of any specific occurrence.

The request is simply that Jesus might be reminded of his companion on the cross at the appropriate time and in the appropriate way. If Jesus could pray for forgiveness on behalf of the people who had crucified them, he would perhaps look favorably upon this petition. There is an unspoken assumption that all will not end for them at death. After this physical death has come, Jesus will perhaps do something in another world or in another dimension of being, and whatever it is, it will be worthwhile to be included. The terrorist appears to be certain that there is something good beyond death in store for Jesus and, therefore by implication, for those who are favored by Jesus.

"*. . . when you come as King.*" The general meaning is clear enough. The terrorist has come to believe that the man on the cross beside him actually is the Messiah, unbelievable as it might seem. On whatever view, the Messiah must have some sort of a kingdom. It is obvious that this Messiah has not yet become the King, however, or he would not be on the cross. Since those who show loyalty to a future king are more likely to be favored than those who wait until after the actual coronation to show their loyalty, he would offer himself now while the Messiah is not yet the King. Beyond this general idea, there are two specific interpretations of these words, each reflected in major English translations, and each based upon a good set of manuscripts.

(1) "*. . . when you come in your kingdom.*" Many of the manuscripts have the preposition as "in." If this reading of the text be adopted, the terrorist is thinking of the Second Coming of Christ to earth for the Final Judgment and the establishment of the eternal Kingdom of God. The return of the Crucified One in royal power and authority would be the focus of the expectation. This interpretation fits Jesus' statement to the high priest that "you will see the Son of Man sitting at the right hand of Power, and coming with the clouds of heaven" (Mark 14:62). This understanding of the text is reflected in RSV ("when you come in your kingly power") and in TEV ("when you come as King."). In this case, the terrorist is asking to be among the dead who are raised to glory when Jesus returns as Messiah. In the meantime, he would expect his soul to wait in some shadowy afterworld. The fact that this vague expectation does not fit Jesus' answer is not really an objection, for there is no necessary connection between his half-formed hope and the reality expressed in Jesus' answer.

(2) "*. . . when you come into your kingdom.*" Many other good manuscripts have "into" as the preposition.

This change of prepositions introduces a very different idea. In this case, the kingdom itself is considered to be in the next world, and the coronation is expected to occur immediately upon passing through physical death. Receiving the spiritual kingdom immediately on the other side of death, of course, does not preclude the later coming in glory at the Parousia. This is the understanding of the text found in KJV and Phillips ("when you come into your kingdom"), NEB ("when you come to your throne"), and NAB ("when you enter upon your reign"). The fact that this does fit Jesus' answer and later Christian theology does not demonstrate that the terrorist understood it at this time.

The arguments and manuscripts are fairly evenly divided. Either text can be defended, and therefore each interpreter is free to select whichever makes the better sense to him or her.

Verse 43. *Jesus said to him, "I promise you that today you will be in Paradise with me."*

"Paradise" was a Persian word which came to mean a private park enclosed by some kind of a wall, and then, specifically, where the king relaxed with his close friends. The word acquired religious importance when the Septuagint chose it to indicate the Garden of Eden in the Genesis story. The association between the Garden of Eden and Paradise became so close that some of the Syriac manuscripts have "in the Garden of Eden" rather than "in Paradise" here. Some of the Old Latin manuscripts have "in the Paradise of the Father" here. Even as the original Garden of Eden was closely associated with God the Father, so the Paradise to which the Son would go is also closely associated with God the Father.

The Garden of Eden became a symbol for the hope that God would ultimately establish his Kingdom upon this earth. "The Lord will comfort Zion and make her wilderness like Eden" (Isaiah 51:3). Since the first Garden of Eden was only for the innocent, sinful humanity was necessarily barred. It can be re-entered, therefore, only by the righteous.

There are three stages in the development of the idea of Paradise as found in this text. First, it was thought that all of the dead souls went to Sheol to await the Final Judgment. The second stage was the separation of Sheol into two parts, Gehenna for the wicked and Paradise for the righteous (2 Esdras 7:36). The Messiah will come to this waiting place and open the gates of Paradise, removing the sword of Adam, and giving the righteous souls to eat of the tree of life (Testament of Levi 18:10-11). The final stage in the concept has the Messiah actually living in Paradise with the souls of the redeemed (2 Corinthians 12:3,4). There is a fitness in this. Since by Adam's sin death entered the world, so by the death of Christ it became possible for the saved to enter the Garden (Romans 5:15) or Paradise. The end is therefore like the beginning. *Endzeit ist Urzeit*

It is clear that in this text Paradise is the place where the souls of the redeemed would enjoy fellowship with the Messiah until the final consummation at the Second Coming. It is virtually synonymous with "heaven," and efforts to distinguish between the two are not successful. This is a definite promise of salvation to the terrorist. Self-consciousness after death is a clear implication of the text also, or else the promise would have no meaning.

The chief problem for interpretation is the chronology involved in the Descent into Hell. If Jesus could promise that "today" you will be with me in Paradise, no room is allowed for the time in the grave or in hell between the death and the resurrection. The preaching to the spirits in prison (1 Peter 3:19) solved two basic problems for Christians: it accounted for the soul of Christ during the time his body was in the grave, and it allowed for an offer of salvation to be given to those who had died before the Incarnation. The idea of going immediately to Paradise seems to contradict this.

In order to avoid this difficulty, some interpreters have altered the punctuation and the reference of "today" from the entrance into Paradise to the time of the promise. "Today I say to you, 'You will enter Paradise with me.'" This, then, leaves open the question as to when the actual entry into Paradise takes place, presumably not until the Ascension. This interpretation, however, then raises the problem of the location of the soul of the terrorist in the meantime. The traditional theology can see the souls of those who will be redeemed in the future, immediately entering Paradise to be with Christ, and the souls of those who are in prison, entering as a group at the appropriate time. The soul of the terrorist would have to accompany Christ to hell, in order then to enter Paradise as part of the group who responded to the preaching.

The contradiction cannot be harmonized in this way, however, for the change in the reference of "today" is contrary to the plain sense of the text. The story of Lazarus and the rich man is evidence that Luke thought of the souls of the redeemed as entering at once into Paradise. The chronological difficulties disappear when we stop trying to visualize these things in the categories of our earthly space and time. If eternity is time-lessness rather than a super unending type of earthly time, the texts can all be read together without contradiction. Eternity must be considered as a dimension of existence beyond the constraints of time. Time belongs to earthly existence, and while we are in this existence, we cannot think except in symbols which belong to this earth. The unearthly dimension cannot be reduced to earthly terms without distortion. It is only when we forget the essentially symbolic nature of language that we can feel difficulty with these texts. In an eternal time-less dimension, perhaps all of these things are simultaneous even though, to the constraints of earthly time, they might have to be sequential.

The Third Word

John 19:25-27

Verse 25. *Standing close to Jesus' cross were his mother, his mother's sister, Mary the wife of Clopas, and Mary Magdalene.*

There is no way to determine how many of the faithful actually remained near the cross. In Luke 23:49, there is the general statement that "all the ones who knew him stood afar off." Presumably Luke included men as well as women, for the "all" is then followed by the specification of a part of the total, "the women who had followed him from Galilee." Matthew simply says that there were "many women" (27:55), and then gives three names (27:56). Any effort to consider the entire tradition must include at least five, and probably six, different women.

"His mother." Mary, the mother of Jesus, plays a strangely minor role in the Passion narrative. This Word from the Cross is her only mention. No Gospel specifically records her presence at the tomb to anoint the body, or on Easter morning, or as having ever received a resurrection appearance. Presumably John took her home, and she remained there until the resurrection. In Acts 1:14, she is at prayer with the Eleven, the other women, and her other sons, the brothers of Jesus. The absence of the brothers at the cross, and their later presence at prayer, suggest that they became believers between these two events. Mary

may have been at the tomb even though she is not mentioned, but there would be no reason to omit her name from the list, and there would be every reason to include it. It may be taken as a firm fact of the tradition, therefore, that she was not there. She may well have been too overcome with grief to be able to handle herself at the tomb. No blame is attached to her absence.

". . . *his mother's sister.*" There is no certain evidence concerning her identity. In Matthew 27:56, three women are named: Mary Magdalene, Mary the mother of James and Joseph, and the mother of the sons of Zebedee. In Mark 15:40, the three are Mary Magdalene, Mary the mother of James the Small and Joses, and Salome. Since they agree on Mary Magdalene and Mary the mother of James and Joseph, it is probable that they agree on the third woman also. This would identify Salome as the mother of the sons of Zebedee. Salome would then be Mary's unnamed sister *if* Mary the wife of Clopas can be identified with Mary the mother of James and Joseph (or Joses); and *if* the names in John are intended to reproduce the three names in Matthew and Mark, with the addition of Mary the mother of Jesus as the fourth woman. In this case, Luke would be drawing upon additional material when he added Joanna and Susanna to the list of the women at the cross. This would make Salome and Zebedee the aunt and uncle of Jesus, and their sons (James and John) would be first cousins to Jesus. This would give a certain logic to Jesus' commitment of his mother to John's care. In Mark 16:1, Salome is with the women who brought spices to anoint the body. She could well have been one to insist that her sister stay home and not go with them. Based upon the existing records, this would seem to be the most probable identification.

There is another possible identification of the unnamed sister, however, if John's text be considered as recording three women at the cross, rather than four. In this case, the unnamed sister would be identified as the wife of Clopas. It is possible to take John's text in this way, but it seems more natural to take four women in two parallel sets, one named and one unnamed. Eusebius has recorded a tradition that Clopas was the brother of Joseph, the father of Jesus. This would make the wife of Clopas Mary's sister-in-law rather than her sister. It is highly unlikely that two sisters would have the same name.

"Mary the wife of Clopas." Nothing certain is known concerning Clopas. In Luke 24:18, a certain Cleopas is named as one of the two disciples in the resurrection appearance on the road to Emmaus. KJV has apparently identified these two by rendering "Cleophas" here. Since the names are far more different in Greek than they appear to be in English, however, it is not probable that the same person is intended.

Matthew 27:56 and Mark 15:40 agree that one of the women was Mary the mother of James and Jospeh (or Joses). The manuscript confusion between the names of "Joseph" and "Joses" in both texts is strong evidence that both names represent the same person. Mark further identifies James by a nickname, "the small." The nickname may refer to his small physical size or to the fact of his being the younger brother, and therefore "smaller" legally and socially. If John has followed the same tradition, it is possible that the wife of Clopas is the mother of James and Joseph. If this is the same James who is mentioned in Matthew 10:3 as the son of Alphaeus, then Clopas and Alphaeus would be the same person. This Mary, identified as the mother of Joses, was with Mary Magdalene watching the burial (Mark 15:47). She would then be "the other Mary" of Matthew 27:61. She also went to the tomb on Easter morning with spices for the anointing of the body (Matthew 28:1 and Mark 16:1).

"Mary Magdalene." She had been tormented by

seven demons until Jesus cast them out (Luke 8:2 and Mark 16:9). The "seven" may be a literal number, but since it was also a numerical symbol for completeness, it may be intended to indicate the seriousness of her condition as one who was completely possessed. She became a devoted Christian from the time of her cure. Nothing is known of her family situation, but she was evidently a woman of means and independent enough of family constraints that she was able to spend much of her time with Jesus and the Twelve and to help with substantial financial support (Luke 8:3 and Mark 15:41). It is the unanimous tradition that she made the final journey to Jerusalem with Jesus, and that she was present at the Crucifixion. She came to the tomb to anoint the body (Mark 16:1 and Luke 23:55 - 24:1), and she reported to the Eleven the fact of the empty tomb and the words of the angels (Luke 24:1-11). Furthermore, she is the only woman in the record who received a personal resurrection appearance (John 20:11-18). She is, therefore, the most important woman in the entire Passion narrative.

Mary Magdalene has often been identified with the unnamed prostitute who anointed Jesus' feet in the house of Simon the Pharisee (Luke 7:36-50). There is a strong tendency for later tradition to supply names for anonymous figures, as we have seen in the case of the two terrorists and will see in the case of the centurion. Since Magdala had a reputation for licentiousness, and since some demon possession could be regarded as related to sinful behavior, it was perhaps inevitable that Mary Magdalene should acquire this reputation in the later tradition. The continuing popularity of this identification is reflected in the modern rock opera, *Jesus Christ, Superstar*. If this had been Luke's understanding, however, it is difficult to see why he would have been so oblique in his references, since such a conversion would not have detracted from her role in the Passion. If the tradition had been early, it is difficult to understand silence on the part of the opponents of Christianity, for it would seem a natural taunt to hurl into the teeth of Christians. It is unlikely that a woman of the social standing of the wife of the steward of Herod Antipas would have been willing to travel in the company of such a notorious prostitute (Luke 8:1-3). In short, there is no evidence at all in the Gospel record that Mary Magdalene had ever had such a shady past.

"Joanna." Although she is not named in John, Luke 24:10 mentions her presence at the empty tomb. This is strong inferential evidence that she was also at the cross. In Luke 8:3, she is described as the wife of Chuza, the steward of Herod Antipas. She was a Galilean woman who had been healed by Jesus of some disease, and subsequently contributed financial support to Jesus and the Twelve. Her husband's attitude is not mentioned, but silence probably indicates that he did not object, or he could have prevented her doing this.

"Susanna." She is not mentioned in any text as actually being at the cross or at the empty tomb. Since Luke 8:3 mentions her as having been healed by Jesus and as having subsequently provided financial support, it is probable that she was part of the unnamed group of Galilean women at the cross.

Verse 26a. *Jesus saw his mother and the disciple he loved standing there;*

Whatever the grouping of the faithful at the cross, it is significant that the beloved disciple has chosen to stand beside Mary, the mother of Jesus. It is not that Jesus' mother and the beloved disciple are both there, but that they are standing side by side. This is brought out more clearly in some of the translations: "standing by her" (Phillips), "standing beside her" (NEB), and "his mother there with the disciple" (NAB). Perhaps he had perceived that a mother's grief might be even more unbearable than the grief of the others, and therefore he had stood beside her to offer what comfort and strength he could for this hour of trial.

The unnamed beloved disciple was next to Jesus at the Last Supper (John 13:23), ran together with Peter to the empty tomb (John 20:4), and was contrasted with Peter in John 21:15-23. The virtually unanimous tradition of the early Church identified this beloved disciple with John the son of Zebedee. If his mother, Salome, can be identified as Mary's sister, then his movement to comfort his aunt is a natural gesture.

Verse 26b. . . . *so he said to his mother, "He is your son."*

The Greek text has: "he said, 'Woman, behold, your son.' " KJV, RSV, and NAB have preserved this text. So many people, however, have an emotional difficulty with "woman" as a term of address in this context that it has been deliberately obscured in a number of translations. Phillips has followed the Old Latin textual tradition in simply omitting the word "woman." NEB has changed "woman" into "mother" even though not a single manuscript shows "mother" in this place. TEV has omitted "woman" in the address and substituted "to his mother." There is no textual warrant for efforts to avoid the plain meaning of the words.

The word "woman" (*gunai*) as a direct address occurs nine times in the Gospels. In the only occurrence which may have any negative overtones, Peter uses the word to the servant girl in the denial scene (Luke 22:57). The angels address Mary Magdalene as "woman" at the empty tomb (John 20:13). The other seven occurrences are on the lips of Jesus himself. Twice Jesus used this word to address women in connection with a healing miracle: once when he healed a woman's daughter (Matthew 15:28), and when he healed a woman herself (Luke 13:12).

Jesus used the word in speaking to the Samaritan woman at the well and then offered her the living water (John 4:21), and to the woman taken in adultery, before telling her that he did not condemn her (John 8:10). Twice he called his mother, "woman": at the wedding in Cana, when she asked him to perform a miracle, (John 2:4), and here.

It is clear, therefore, that "woman" on the lips of Jesus, as a form of address, is not unfeeling harshness. On the contrary, it is always the prelude to some special mark of regard. The apparent harshness could only come in the sense that he addresses his mother as he would address any other woman. The special claim which a mother might expect to have upon her son seems to have been consistently denied by Jesus from the beginning of the public ministry. It is perhaps true that Mary would have a more difficult time than any other in coming to a true faith in Jesus as the Messiah, for she was required to lose her son emotionally if she was to gain her Savior. In spite of the signs associated with the birth, she had first changed his diapers, and then was required to learn to see him as the Messiah of Israel. The quality of her ultimate faith and religious maturity is best seen in her ability at last to make this transition in attitude, not in her difficulty in doing so. It may have hurt her to hear Jesus comment that whoever does the will of God is his brother and sister and mother (Mark 3:35); and to hear him reply to the woman who affirmed that the womb which bore him was blessed, that rather the ones who hear the word of God are blessed (Luke 11:27ff.). It was a necessary part of her growth, however, at last to realize that she stood in the same relationship to Jesus as any other human being, a sinner seeking salvation.

Jesus must have recognized Mary's peculiar difficulty in this regard, and therefore consistently moved her in this direction. There is, therefore, a tenderness displayed even in this use of the word "woman" at this time. It is

44

theologically important to retain the word in translation here, but in context, it also reveals Jesus' concern for her earthly welfare. The last responsible act of kindness he can do for her earthly life is to provide for her support and protective custody at the hands of one of his disciples. At the same time, she must see here more than the painful death of her son. This is the act of atonement in progress. The picture of Mary praying in Acts with the others, together with her other children and the Eleven, is evidence that she did in fact make the transition from Jesus her son to Jesus the Christ.

Verse 27. *Then he said to the disciple, "She is your mother." From that hour the disciple took her to live in his home.*

John and Mary both accepted Jesus' command. "From that hour" most probably does not mean that they left the scene of the Crucifixion before it was over, but that when she did leave the site, it was to go with John to his home rather than to her own home. The absence of her other children, and the fact that Jesus wanted her with John rather than with any of them, is an additional illustration of the greater importance of spiritual relationships than ties of blood.

Except for the single mention of Mary at prayer with the others in Acts, nothing is known of her future. Two separate traditions developed about her. In one tradition she lived with John in Jerusalem until her death. The other tradition had her move to Ephesus with John. The grave of John at Ephesus is still shown to tourists, but there is no tradition of Mary's grave at Ephesus.

The Fourth Word

Mark 15:33-36

Verse 33. *At noon the whole country was covered with darkness, which lasted for three hours.*

"At noon . . . which lasted for three hours." The Greek text has from the sixth to the ninth hours, from noon until 3:00 p.m. This is the basis for the Good Friday Service of the Words from the Cross. Since "three" was a common Christian symbol for God, it is possible that there is theological significance in the time span, indicating that this darkness was of God and not a natural phenomenon. The "three" appears again in the days the body of Jesus lay in the grave. Darkness symbolized death and the grave, among other things, and therefore it is possible that there is an intentional connection between the two. The three hours of darkness may anticipate typologically the three days in the grave. The fact that darkness can symbolize Hell itself as well as death makes possible the further connection with the Descent into Hell.

It is significant that the darkness began at noon. It is the midpoint of the six hours Jesus was upon the cross. During the first three hours, according to Mark, there were no signs that this was more than the execution of an ordinary man. In the second three hours, however, something else began to appear in the darkness: the cry of dereliction, the association of the crowd with the cry to

Elijah, the rending of the veil of the temple, and the confession of the centurion at the foot of the cross. To Mark, therefore, the darkness introduced the manifestation of the power of God into the crucifixion scene.

As the mid-point of the day, "noon" symbolizes the strength of the sun, and therefore symbolically can indicate the height of any kind of power. Amos 8:9 is commonly associated with this darkness. Speaking of the judgment of God upon the people, Amos said that on that day God will make the sun go down at noon, and darken the earth in broad daylight. At the height of their self-confidence in their own power, the brightness of the noon sun will disappear and they will know that judgment has come upon them. At the crucifixion, at the noon time, when the power of evil was at the height, when it seemed triumphant, the sudden darkness revealed the power of God.

"... *the whole country.* " The Greek has "the whole earth." This has been understood in two ways. (1) It may be restricted to Judea or to Jerusalem and its surrounding area. This understanding seems to be reflected in the standard translations: "the whole land" (KJV, RSV, and NEB), "the whole countryside" (Phillips and NAB), and "the whole country" (TEV). This is required for a common understanding of the darkness as the result of a storm. The black sirocco is a hot wind from the south-east which blackens the sky as it rages over the land. In this case, the supernatural element of the darkness would be confined to coincidence. The hand of God brought the storm at the significant moment, and it lasted precisely the fitting period of time. (2) The darkness has been understood to cover "the whole earth." The RSV offers this translation in the margin. In this case, the storm does not offer a sufficient explanation. The alternative has been to consider an eclipse of the sun affecting a larger area. At least from the third century, however, it has been pointed out that an eclipse of the sun at the time of the Passover is astronomically impossible. An eclipse, therefore, would require a more direct supernatural aspect. In this case, God would not be able to work through nature, but would have to suspend the laws of nature, and the result would be an undeniable miracle of greater proportions than a storm with a natural explanation.

If Mark meant that a storm, of whatever proportions, had struck the area at that time with such theological significance, it is hard to believe that he would not have said so. Storms are associated with the power of God as much as darkness is. The advantage of the storm is that it allows the miraculous element to be muted somewhat. The miracle upon which Christian faith is based, however, is that a risen Savior has offered to extend the power of that resurrection to any who desire it. If this miracle is accepted, it is hard to see why the lesser miracle associated with the darkness would be a problem. If that miracle is not accepted, the biblical record is not meaningful anyway.

Any miracle in the biblical record is a sign pointing to something else. The darkness points to a divine involvement in the events of the cross in a mysterious and complete way. If this is so, then it is a supernatural event, and the means are not important. If an eclipse was not astronomically possible at the time, God could still have suspended such laws. The meaning of the darkness in the record is determinative at this point. If the death of Jesus the Christ on the cross was a truly unique event, and if the darkness is indeed supernaturally associated with it, then a cosmic darkness for the world is more meaningful than a localized darkness for Jerusalem or Judea. Therefore, it is more probable that Mark intended a quiet thick darkness over the whole world, than that he intended a localized darkness or a storm.

"*. . . was covered with darkness.*" In physical

terms, darkness is a negative absence of light rather than a positive force in its own right. My only experience with absolute darkness was in a part of an underground cave which had been specially prepared. Under such conditions, the darkness seems to acquire a positive power in its own right. The darkness begins to appear as a "something" surrounding one. This is the experience of darkness described in Exodus 10:21-23. The darkness which came upon the Egyptians as a judgment of God could be "felt." By contrast, Israel remained in the light. There is an inescapable typology between the three days of darkness, the three hours of darkness, and the three days in the tomb.

Light and darkness are used in many different ways in the Bible, but always God is beyond both. Darkness is death and light is life. Darkness is Hell and light is Heaven. Darkness is evil and light is good. The darkness in the creation story, however, is perhaps more closely related to the darkness in our text. The materials have been created to produce the heavens and the earth, but they have not yet been shaped into any recognizable form. The darkness which was upon the face of the deep (Genesis 1:2) is related to Chaos, which is kept back by the continuing creative power of God, but is always ready to slip the leash and once again reduce the world to formlessness. If the mind is darkened when God leaves it alone (Romans 1:21), the world also might be darkened by God's withdrawal for a time without the need to think of storms or eclipses as explanations.

Darkness is a sign of the approaching judgment of God in Isaiah 50:3 and Jeremiah 15:9. In Matthew 24:29 and Mark 13:24, the darkness is a sign of the final judgment and the end of the world. In all of these cases, the darkness is cosmic and eschatological rather than simply physical. It seems clear that the darkness associated with the Crucifixion is more than physical, and is to be interpreted along these lines. It is not the prelude to the end of the world, as in these texts, for the world has in fact continued to exist. These texts, however, help, because this darkness ties the Passion into the ultimate plan of God in its cosmic and eschatological sense. The darkness in this context, therefore, is a sign that this death has an ultimate saving significance for the whole world, past as well as future. If an individual attitude towards this death is to have eschatological significance, the darkness associated with judgment is a fitting accompaniment of the death. The horizontal dimension of the darkness, therefore, is significant as covering the entire world.

The darkness also has a vertical dimension, however, which includes the ideas of sin, death, and even Hell as the absence of God. In this sense, the darkness is part of the completeness of the death. If the atoning death is to be real, it must include not only physical death, but even the experience of Hell itself under the condemnation of sin. This is the profound reality of the cry of dereliction in this Word from the Cross. The darkness, therefore, is part of the judgment of God against the One on the cross who bore at that moment the sins of the world. That darkness is centered on the cross, but includes at that time all of humanity. The terrible danger at that particular moment was that the Christ may decide not to go through with it after all. The darkness could be lifted at the actual death, for then it was accomplished once and for all. That the Christ would do this has been so inconceivable that persistent efforts have been made to mute the experience. An early heresy held that Christ only appeared to suffer. The powerful novel by Nikos Kazantsakis, *The Last Temptation of Christ*, deals precisely with this theme. This interpretation of the theological dimension of the darkness fits the terrible struggle at Gethsemane in which Jesus at last came to make the decision to go through with the sacrifice. It also fits the Gospel understanding of the Passion as a voluntary sacrifice rather than as a tragic miscarriage of justice. This is the ultimate completion of the Incarnation.

> Verse 34. *At three o'clock Jesus cried out with a loud shout, "Eloi, Eloi, lema sabachthani?" which means, My God, my God, why did you abandon me?"*

"At three o'clock Jesus cried out with a loud shout." In both Matthew and Mark, the two who record this word, the tradition is firm that it was uttered in a loud voice. Therefore, it would have been heard by all who were standing by. Only three times in the New Testament is this particular phrase used ("cried out with a loud voice"): here and in Matthew 27:46 in the same context, and in Acts 8:7 when demons leave a human body. Other occurrences which seem the same in English translations use different Greek verbs. This verb occurs only twelve times in the entire New Testament. Leaving aside the references to the voice crying in the wilderness to prepare the way of the Lord, and cases of unruly crowds shouting to government officials, there are three additional uses which might be compared. Twice the word is used of prayer, once of a blind man calling to Jesus for mercy (Luke 18:38), and once of the elect calling upon God (Luke 18:7). Galatians 4:27 quotes Isaiah 54:1 in a context of God's mercy. There are, therefore, parallels in usage for a cry of despair and for a desperate cry in faith to God for help. The verb can support either of the main interpretations of the cry from the cross. It is interesting to note, however, that John does not record a loud cry from the cross at all, and Luke 23:46 (before the committal word) uses a different verb.

"Eloi, Eloi, lema sabachthani?" The variation to be found in the translations here and in Matthew 27:46 is due to the mixture of Hebrew and Aramaic in virtually

all of the manuscripts. The Hebrew of Psalms 22:1 would be: "Eli, Eli, lama sabachthani?" This is reflected in the translation of KJV, RSV, Phillips, and NEB of Matthew 27:46. It has been made to reflect the Hebrew, however, for even in it the manuscripts reflect the mixture of languages.

"Eli, Eli" is found in the best manuscripts in Matthew 27:46, but two of the best have the Aramaic "Eloi, Eloi." "Eloi, Eloi" is found in the best manuscripts in Mark, but several have "Eli, Eli." There is similar confusion between the Hebrew "lama" and the Aramaic "lema" in both places. There is general agreement concerning "sabachthani" in both places, although some manuscripts have different spellings.

This mixture of Hebrew and Aramaic makes it difficult to determine exactly what Jesus said. He may have quoted the Hebrew, or he may have said it in Aramaic. The meaning, of course, is not affected.

"... *sabachthani.*" This is a loose spelling in Greek of a Hebrew verb which means to abandon, forsake, or leave in a wide variety of settings. A man may abandon his wife in a divorce action, or his fields so they are not tilled, or a claim to something, or advice, or even his anger. A man may set free some one or some thing from some sort of bondage, or leave something for some one else to do. A lion may even abandon or forsake his thicket. Of more interest, however, is the usage in which men abandon their idols or abandon God, and in which God abandons men, or his anger, or does not abandon his promise. When people feel that God has abandoned the land, they feel free to commit crimes (Ezekiel 8:12). When the people abandoned God in idolatry, he abandoned them, and so they fell into the hand of their enemy Shishak (2 Chronicles 12:5). It may seem as if God has abandoned a person (Isaiah 49:14), but after a brief abandonment God will gather his people again with great compassion (Isaiah 54:7). There is the conviction that God will not abandon the poor and the needy (Isaiah 41:17), and has not forsaken his people even in their bondage (Ezra 9:9). An individual believer is sure that God has not abandoned his soul to Sheol (Psalms 16:10).

Of the greatest interest for this text, however, is Deuteronomy 31:17. Near the end of his life, Moses received a revelation from God in which God said that the people would break the covenant in idolatry, and in response, God's anger will be kindled against them, and "I will forsake them and hide my face from them, and they will be devoured." This is the idea of God's turning his face from sin and is the source of the common idea that when Christ took the sin of the world upon himself at the cross the Father had to look away from him, and that triggered the cry of dereliction.

Psalms 22:1 is a cry that God has abandoned his faithful one into the hands of his enemies and has not answered prayer for deliverance. Christians saw in this psalm the prophecy of the Christ. In verses 7-8 they saw the mockery at the cross, in verse 16 the piercing of hands and feet, and in verse 18 the gambling for the clothing. The psalm goes on to make an affirmation of faith that God will deliver a people yet unborn.

". . . *which means, 'My God, my God, why did you abandon me?'* " The Greek verb is an accurate translation of the Hebrew verb. The prevailing idea within the verb is to "leave in the lurch." An Egyptian papyrus, dated within theNew Testament period, has the verb in the sense of "he deserted me, leaving me in a state of destitution." In 2 Corinthians 4:9, Christians are "persecuted but not forsaken." Hebrews 13:5 affirms that God will never forsake his people. This is echoed in the Testament of Joseph 2:4, "For the Lord does not forsake them that fear him."

This Word from the Cross is the most difficult of them all to interpret. It has the potential of being deeply troubling to people. If Luke and John knew the word, they omitted it from their account. One Greek and three Old Latin manuscripts have apparently changed the text to avoid difficulty in interpretation. They have, "My God, my God, why have you (allowed the crowd to) mocked me?" If the reference should be to God mocking Jesus, it is even more difficult. The reference, therefore, must be to God's allowing the crowd to mock or revile. The Word then would be tied to the necessity of the Passion in general. Four major interpretations of the text, found in most manuscripts, should be mentioned.

(1) *It really is an affirmation of faith in the Father.* There is some evidence that a quotation of the opening verse of a passage implied the entire passage. The difficulty of loud speech from a cross would naturally preclude quoting the entirety of Psalms 22. The progression of idea in the psalm is from despair and ill-treatment at the hands of enemies to a triumphant affirmation of faith in God. If Jesus were to make such an affirmation of triumphant faith under such circumstances, he could do no better than the words of this psalm. Therefore, what is apparently a cry of despair is in reality an affirmation of faith which would have a strengthening effect upon those who heard it. This is probably the most popular interpretation. Its advantage is that it turns a difficult statement into a thrilling statement of hope. If this were the plain and obvious meaning, however, it is difficult to see why so many people through the centuries have been troubled by it. Furthermore, if this were the obvious intent of the saying, it is easy to see how later tradition would have supplied the saying to make a Messianic psalm have the authority of Jesus behind its interpretation. The expectation that Jesus would display this kind of consistent faith reduces the power and profundity of the saying. It is not possible to know what was in the mind of Jesus during this time, and we are not free to speculate. We can only deal with the record as it has been

preserved. Finally, if the intent of the saying was to strengthen listeners, it is strange that it was addressed to God rather than to the by-standers. There is nothing in the record to support this interpretation.

(2) *It is a cry for help.* The meaning of the psalm is not so much the absence of God as the failure of God to render assistance. Since the psalmist goes on to express his conviction that God will ultimately give the needed help, the quotation of this verse is in reality a prayer for help in this difficult moment. This fits with the agony in Gethsemane in which Jesus showed a natural reluctance to drink this cup. Even if it should be God's will that this be the cup, now that it is at the lips, is there no way that it can be withdrawn, consistent with God's purpose? The crowd interpreted this also as a cry for help, but mistakenly thought that Jesus was calling upon Elijah for deliverance. This interpretation takes more seriously the agony than does the first, and explains why the cry is addressed to God rather than to the by-standers. It takes the psalm seriously. This interpretation also takes seriously the essential difficulty of the saying, for a cry for deliverance from the cross is as disturbing as the prayer in Gethsemane.

(3) *God is obscured for the moment.* There was no Godforsakenness in reality, even for this moment, but the perception of God's presence was blunted. The crushing experience of receiving the sins of the world upon an essential holiness and sinlessness produced a desolation of spirit in which the communion the Son had always known with the Father appeared to be broken. This interpretation takes seriously the plain meaning of the words and the sense of despair and aloneness behind them. It is less troubling, however, because it preserves a theological affirmation that the Father in reality was never absent and was totally involved in the Passion. This fits the Gospel record. It fits the incarnation with the other evidences of the weakness of the flesh.

(4) *It is a genuine cry of dereliction.* The Lutheran and Calvinist theological traditions have generally seen this as an accurate recognition that at this moment the Son had been forsaken by the Father. If the cross represented atonement as substitution, and if Jesus really took the sins of the world upon himself, and bore the penalty — then the penalty must be complete. The penalty for sin is not simply the death of the body, but also the death of the soul in the sense of separation from God. Only through this complete and unfathomable Godforsakenness, could Christ truly take the place of sinful men and women. If the Christ was fully human, then he had to bear the full penalty, not even knowing how it would all come out. Anything less than this would make a caricature out of the Incarnation. Such a cry of dereliction fits the Incarnation completely. It has been objected that this interpretation obscures the involvement of the Father in the Passion, and is contrary to the love of God. The passages dealing with God's never abandoning his people, however, do not relate specifically to the Messiah. The uniqueness of this experience makes any other passages beside the point. If the holiness of God forced him to abandon his Son to the consequences of sin, the deepest love possible, even for God, would be displayed and not denied. In the plan of salvation, Father and Son each had required roles to play, and therefore even the forsaking is part of the complete participation of the Father in the Passion. If the Christ was fully God, however, so that the substitution had value, there would be a recognition that even suffering at this depth is God's work. The quotation of the psalm, therefore, represents the faith that the Godforsakenness is not necessarily permanent. This takes seriously the plain meaning of the words in the situation, but also reminds the reader that, even at this point, Father and Son are mutually involved. The note of victory in the

psalm could be seen only after-the-fact in the post resurrection era. While certainty in interpretation is not possible, this interpretation offers the best theological congruence with the total concept of Incarnation and Atonement. It also best accounts for the disturbing difficulty people have with this saying, for the tendency is to exalt the divine in Jesus and soften the human.

Verse 35. *Some of the people there heard him and said, "Listen, he is calling for Elijah!"*

At this point the question of the objective reality of the darkness must be considered. Matthew, Mark, and Luke agree that the darkness lasted from noon until 3:00 p.m. and that it was a time of silence. The cry of dereliction immediately follows the lifting of the darkness. Presumably the following actions and words take place in relatively rapid sequence, and the death occurs soon after 3:00 p.m. The crowd is at the cross before the onset of the darkness and is still there when the darkness is lifted. If the darkness had been caused by the howling of a black sirocco storm, it is incredible that the people would not have run for shelter. It is further incredible that they would have been at the cross again immediately upon the cessation of the storm, as if nothing had happened. If the darkness had been the thick "felt" kind of the Egyptian plague, it is incredible that there was no panic or confusion. The people simply do not react to the darkness in any way. On the "realistic" level of the reading which would have registered on a light meter, the only darkness which is credible is an overcast sky. This would so dilute the theological meaning of the darkness that it would not have been worth mentioning at all.

It is evident, therefore, that this darkness would not have registered upon a light meter. This darkness is of cosmic significance and of God's realm. It is, therefore, visible only to the eye of faith. It is not "real" to the nonbeliever. For the Christian, however, this is a deeper and more profound reality than any mere passing physical darkness would be. It is yet another example of the interpenetration of this world and the world to come which is a basic premise of the gospel record. John 5:24 may serve as a specific example. Jesus said that whoever comes to faith has already crossed over from death into life. Even while continuing under the physical constraints of the flesh, and with a physical death yet to face, the believer is already in eternal life. Are we to say that this eternal life is not "real" because it is not apparent to the eye of the nonbeliever and is not subject to verification in a biological laboratory? The darkness has the same sort of reality. This allows the interpreter to take seriously the theological significance of the darkness, and yet understand the actions of the people at the cross. To be concerned about the "light meter reality" of the darkness is to fail to take Mark seriously.

"*. . . he calls Elijah.*" One old Latin manuscript seems to put this in the mouth of the soldiers by reading: "he calls the Sun." Pagan soldiers would then consider that Jesus was appealing for help to Apollo, the sun-god. It is extremely unlikely, however, that the genuine tradition would be preserved only in a single manuscript. The soldiers would not be likely to have understood "Elijah," and so the by-standers must have been Jews. It is possible that either "Eli" or "Eloi" could have been misunderstood as "Elijah," but it was more likely a deliberate pun as part of the mockery. The rulers had taunted Jesus with his inability to save himself. Now the taunt is the refusal of Elijah to save him.

Elijah was associated with the Messiah and the final consummation of the world in a persistent, though varying, tradition. The ultimate basis of the tradition is the mysterious translation of Elijah into heaven by a whirlwind associated with a chariot of fire drawn by horses of fire (2 Kings 2:11). 1 Maccabees 2:58 affirms that this happened because of Elijah's great zeal for the law.

Malachi 4:5 fixed Elijah as the messenger whom God would send before the great and terrible day of the Lord. In his return, Elijah would purify the priesthood (Malachi 3:3,4) and bring peace by turning the hearts of the fathers and children towards each other (Malachi 4:6). Sirach 48:10 defined this as calming the wrath of God before it breaks out in fury, and adds the restoration of the tribes of Jacob as an additional task of Elijah upon his return. The coming of Elijah, therefore, will announce the time of preparation for the immediate coming of the Messiah. If Elijah has not come, the Messiah cannot have come.

When the tradition affirmed two forerunners, one of them must be Elijah. When two holy men returned, the end was near. In 4 Esdras 6:26, the hearts of those who dwell upon the earth will be changed when the men will appear "who were translated, who did not taste death." This could refer to Enoch, Moses, and Elijah. In the Transfiguration, Moses and Elijah appeared to Jesus. The disciples asked Jesus why the scribes say that Elijah must come before the Messiah comes (Matthew 17:10 and Mark 9:11). Moses may have appeared because of the prophecy of Deuteronomy 18:15, about the appearance of a prophet like Moses. Elijah appeared as the necessary fore-runner of the Messiah. The two witnesses of Revelation 11:3 are most likely to be identified as Moses and Elijah in this connection. In this tradition they are martyred, and then have a share in the conquest of the Antichrist.

The Transfiguration seems to know the tradition that Elijah would suffer as the forerunner of the Messiah. The tradition recorded in Revelation expects Moses and Elijah to suffer in the future as part of the final consummation. The contradiction of the gospel account is more apparent than real. In Matthew 11:14, Jesus explicitly identified John the Baptizer as the Elijah of Malachi 4:5. It is not a reincarnation of the actual Elijah, however, but the Elijah mission which was fulfilled in the call to repentance and the ministry of preparation. This means that Elijah has already come, and Elijah talks with Jesus about the coming passion in Jerusalem (Luke 9:31). Since the spirit of Elijah in John the Baptizer has fulfilled the prophecy regarding the necessary forerunner, it is possible for Jesus to be considered as the Messiah. At the same time, Moses and Elijah may be the two witnesses who are to come in connection with the final consummation. Perhaps it was not until the delay lengthened between the resurrection and the parousia, that Elijah could be seen in both roles, as the necessary forerunner of the Messiah, and also as the future eschatological figure associated with the final return of Christ.

Christians who had understood John the Baptizer as Elijah had then identified Jesus as the Messiah. If Elijah as the forerunner can be understood in connection with suffering, then a suffering Messiah might be understood as well. It is clear, however, that Elijah was also seen in terms of triumph. Jews who did not expect a suffering Messiah would not expect a suffering forerunner. Therefore Elijah was yet to come. The taunt in this verse would then imply an objective test of Jesus' Messianic claims: if Elijah comes to take him off the cross, they will have evidence that Jesus is the Messiah. If Elijah does not come to take him off the cross, on the other hand, they will have additional evidence that Jesus is not the Messiah.

Verse 36a. *One of them ran up with a sponge, soaked it in cheap wine, and put it on the end of a stick.*

The tradition is firm that some one filled a sponge with cheap wine, jammed it on the end of a reed or a stick or a staff, and then held it up to Jesus' lips so that he could bite on the sponge and thereby get some of the liquid in his mouth. In John 19:30, Jesus accepts the drink, but "they" rather than "some one" offer the drink, and no words concerning Elijah are spoken. In Matthew 27:48, one of the bystanders offers the drink, but does not say anything. Luke 23:36 records the first mocking drink offered by the soldiers, which Jesus refuses, but does not mention this drink. A Jew would probably not have been allowed by the soldiers to approach the cross in this way, and so most likely it was a soldier who offered the wine. The alteration in the tradition between singular and plural can probably be accounted for on the supposition that one soldier actually held it up to the lips of Jesus, but that the others had shared in the decision to do this and in the preparation of the sponge.

Verse 36b. *Then he held it up to Jesus' lips and said: "Wait! Let us see if Elijah is coming to bring him down from the cross!"*

There are two ways in which Mark's text can be understood.

(1) The soldier may have been filled with compassion for the suffering of Jesus and desired to do this as an act of kindness, but he feared that the hostility of the crowd was such that such an act of kindness might trigger an angry response. Therefore, as a way around the hostility of the crowd, he picked up the Elijah mockery and pretended to go along with it. "Allow" (me to give him the wine); (then by keeping him conscious for a longer time) "let us see if Elijah will come." The strength of this interpretation is that it allows an act of compassion, consistent with John's account, to be preserved at the same time that the Elijah mockery is recognized. The

Greek words allow this interpretation. The chief problem with this interpretation is that it requires a great many assumptions. On balance, the idea that the soldier manipulated a hostile crowd in order to perform a compassionate act seems too subtle to be a credible report of the soldier's intention.

(2) It is possible that the motivation was not compassion at all, but rather was an essentially hostile desire to prolong the agony as much as possible in order to enjoy the show. The word translated as "allow" would have been absorbed into the phrase, and the meaning would be simply: "let us see." The soldier would then have joined in fully with the Elijah mockery, whether he really understood it or not. A rough Roman soldier would be fully capable of this. The problem is that it contradicts the implications of the account in John.

The words about Elijah, as spoken by the soldier, appear to present an insoluble problem for exegesis. In Matthew 27:48-49, the person who actually offered the drink, whether a soldier or a Jew, does not say anything at all. It is the crowd which shouts: "stop (do not give him the wine); let us see if Elijah will come to rescue him." This would appear to represent more accurately what actually happened, than Mark's placement of the words in the soldier's mouth.

The most probable explanation of the problem as a whole is that a lot was going on, and that it was remembered differently. Jesus may well have simply said to the soldiers, "I thirst," and they may well have responded simply and compassionately to the request (as in John). There may have been no real connection between the Elijah mockery and the offering of the drink. The Elijah mockery would then be considered as belonging essentially to the cry of dereliction rather than to the offering of the drink. The soldiers and Jesus would not be paying attention to the Elijah mockery in the request for and the offer of the drink, even if it was going on at the same time. In Matthew, these two actions can yet be separated. In Mark, however, the two actions have become welded together into a single action by having the soldier echo the Elijah mockery. In the tradition followed by Mark, it is probable that the Elijah mockery was charged with such theological and prophetic meaning that it dominated the entire scene. Even though the drink was remembered, the Elijah motif swallowed up the simple act of compassion, and they became fused.

The Fifth Word

John 19:28-29

Verse 28. *Jesus knew that by now everything had been completed; and in order to make the scripture come true, he said, "I am thirsty."*

"After this." These words, in the Greek text and rendered in most English translations, have been omitted by TEV. John's account does not offer specific time references, affirming only that the crucifixion was completed during the daylight hours. From Mark we know that the crucifixion began at 9:00 a.m. Matthew, Mark, and Luke specify that the darkness lasted from noon until 3:00 p.m. The time of death is not specified in any of the accounts, but it is usually inferred that it occurred shortly after 3:00 p.m. The reference here is not to time but to the relative sequence of events. This word was spoken after the word of adoption to Mary and John.

"Jesus knew." The translations vary between "knowing" or "knew" (KJV, RSV, and TEV), "realizing" (Phillips and NAB), and "aware" (NEB). The point is the deliberate self-consciousness with which Jesus knew that everything necessary had now been done. This is another reminder that Jesus was in control of the situation, and not merely a passive victim.

". . . that by now everything had been completed." There is some variation in translation: "accomplished" (KJV), "finished" (RSV and NAB), "completed" (Phillips and TEV), and "come to its

appointed end" (NEB). The Greek verb is related to the noun, "end" or "purpose," from which teleology has come into English. It can mean "to finish" or "complete" or "to end." The passive can be used as a way of indicating that God has completed all of these things, and therefore would be a reminder that what has happened here was planned and foreordained through all eternity. It was, therefore, a voluntary sacrifice in which Father and Son co-operated, and not a tragic miscarriage of justice or a murder. The verb is in the present perfect tense, which indicates a past action whose results continue into the present. The theological implication of the tense, therefore, is that the effects of that "completion" are of continuing value to the reader. Everything required in order to accomplish an atonement has now been finished. The point of no return has been passed. The remainder will now unfold according to the divine will. Jesus has done his job. The Father will do the rest.

It is possible to take the next phrase with this phrase: "everything had been completed, in order that the Scripture might be fulfilled." This would give a good logical sense, but it leaves "I thirst" hanging. It is better, therefore, to take "in order that the Scripture might be fulfilled" as the introduction to "I thirst." The implication is that the remaining words are not as vital to the work of atonement as what has preceded.

This verb is not the common one for the fulfilling or completing of what has been written in the Scriptures, and therefore it is possible that the reference here is to the total complex of the Incarnation, to include the ministry as well as the Passion. Since this was all written in Scripture, however, it is hard to avoid the intense sense of the necessity being grounded in the written prophecy, even though the written prophecy may be conceived as grounded in the eternal will of God. Paul used this verb in the sense of the fulfillment of Scripture in his sermon in the synagogue in Antioch of Pisidia:

"and when they had fulfilled all that was written of him, they took him down from the tree and laid him in a tomb" (Acts 13:29).

"*. . . and in order to make the Scripture come true.*" The other translations have some form of "fulfill" or "fulfillment." This verb is cognate with the one translated as "finished" or "completed" in the previous phrase. There is considerable overlapping of meaning in the two verbs, but this one seems to have a stronger sense of bringing something to an end by fulfilling its purpose. This verb is especially used within the context of the fulfillment of prophecy. It is the final event of the Crucifixion to which there is a direct prophetic reference in the Old Testament. A prophecy is not considered to be fulfilled until it has been actualized in such a concrete way. John could not conceive that such a prophecy would not be fulfilled at this time. Therefore, he interprets the thirst as being "in order to" or "for the purpose of" making the prophecy come true.

It is not possible to be certain whether John thought that Jesus deliberately spoke the word in order to make sure that the prophecy came true in a causal connection, or whether the natural thirst which Jesus felt and mentioned unconsciously fulfilled the prophecy. In either case, the prophecy was fulfilled, and that was the important point. It is over-subtle to see significance in the placement of this particular Word from the Cross, as if Jesus had not felt free to mention his physical thirst until after everything had first been completed for others lest it be selfishness on his part. The connection with the fulfillment of prophecy is too close for such psychological interpreting. It is also idle to speculate that Jesus needed the assistance of a drink for his parched vocal cords in order to be able to speak the remaining Words from the Cross. This may well be true from a physiological point of view, but it has no relevance. The action had to occur because it had been prophesied. No other reason is necessary.

"... *he said, 'I am thirsty.'* " Three Old Testament texts are possibilities for the prophecy which is fulfilled. The reference may be to Psalms 22:15, "my strength is dried up like a potsherd, and my tongue cleaves to my jaws." In view of the many other details from this psalm which were seen as prophesying the crucifixion, this is possible. It is a description of the suffering which produces the thirst, however, more than a statement that the thirst will be relieved. The same objection applies to Psalms 69:3, "I am weary with crying; my throat is parched." The most probable reference is Psalms 69:21, "they gave me poison (or gall) for food, and for my thirst they gave me vinegar to drink." This text suggests not only the thirst, but also an action by others which is triggered by the thirst.

It is difficult to know whether John saw a loose correspondence between prophecy and fulfillment, or whether he intended a more exact fit. The context of Psalms 69:21 demands a bitter or poisonous food and a sour or nauseous vinegar. In the psalm an insult is definitely intended. The sufferer is mocked with a bitter herb instead of with bread, and with vinegar instead of with wine. It does not seem likely that the soldiers would have vinegar with them in order that an exact fit might come with the prophecy. They would have brought cheap wine with them. In general, the offer of the cheap wine is considered to be an act of kindness intended to relieve suffering. This would require a loose correspondence between prophecy and fulfillment rather than an exact fit. The fact that Jesus accepted the drink also suggests that it was intended and received as an act of kindness. Matthew 27:34 may record a different fulfillment of the prophecy with a closer correspondence to the context of the psalm. The wine mingled with gall may be closer to the bitter or poisonous food and the sour vinegar. The situations seem sufficiently different to conclude that two different drinks are being offered, rather than considering them to be varying traditions of the same drink, and therefore the prophecy may be considered as fulfilled in each case. The fact that Jesus refused the first drink does not mean that the prophecy was not fulfilled, for they "gave" him the drink.

In addition to the fulfillment of prophecy, the total meaning of the thirst and the drink must include the thought of the weakness of the flesh as a part of the completeness of the Incarnation. This close to death, the punished body makes itself known with such a painful insistence that this cry of weakness is torn from Jesus' throat, perhaps almost as a groan. There is a dreadful irony between this cry of thirst and the promised ability to give living water which will forever quench thirst (John 4:14), and the affirmation that anyone who thirsts may come to Jesus for the drink of living water (John 7:37-38). Now he is dependent for a drink upon the kindness of the soldiers.

Verse 29. *A bowl was there, full of cheap wine; so a sponge was soaked in the wine, put on a stalk of hyssop, and lifted up to his lips.*

"A bowl was there, full of cheap wine." The variation in translation between "vessel" (KJV), "bowl" (RSV, Phillips, and TEV), and "jar" (NEB and NAB) reflects the difficulty in determining the exact nature of the container. The Greek word can mean any of these and some others as well. All that can be said for certain is that it was a container which could hold liquid, and with a wide enough neck or top that a sponge could be dipped into the liquid. Only in this text in the Gospel accounts of this scene is the container mentioned. The soldiers may have brought the wine to help pass the time, but because the hyssop and sponge are ready to hand, it seems more likely that it had been brought specifically for the men on the crosses. If so, the offer of the drink may have been

an expected or routine part of the process, a "standard operating procedure." In this case, the giving of the drink may simply be neutral with no overtones of kindness. Even if this is so, however, it could also be done with kindly intent. All we can be sure of from John's account is that it was not part of the mockery.

"... *so a sponge was soaked in the wine, put on a stalk of hyssop, and lifted up to his lips.*" The intended action is clear enough, but the hyssop does not really seem to be an appropriate instrument for lifting the sponge to Jesus' lips. The cross would have to be high enough to lift the feet off the ground, but need not lift the feet very high. It is probable that an average sized man would be able to reach up to Jesus' mouth. A long stick or reed, therefore, need not be envisioned. Probably the cross would not have been made any larger or higher than necessary in order to do its job.

The hyssop is now commonly identified with the Syrian marjoram, although older commentators often state that it has not been identified. The Syrian marjoram is a shrub, one to two feet high, with slender branches and wooly-haired leaves. It is valued for its aroma, which is similar to that of mint. The slender branches can be cut and formed into bunches to be used as sprinklers. In 1 Kings 4:33, the hyssop is opposed to the cedar as the smallest shrub to the mightiest tree of the forest. Since Matthew 27:48 and Mark 15:36 mention a reed or a stick or a rod, and since the common identification of the hyssop plant is not easy to visualize in this way, a number of solutions have been offered.

One seventh or eighth century manuscript eliminated the problem completely by changing the "hyssop" of this text to the "reed" of Matthew and Mark. The tendency among the scribes was to make the Gospels agree with each other, and therefore any change of the text in this direction is suspect. Another tendency of scribes was to eliminate problems by substituting an easier text for a more difficult one. Since "hyssop" in this context is more difficult to understand than "reed," this manuscript offers a commentary on the text rather than the correct reading.

An eleventh century manuscript solved the problem with a simpler change in the text. Instead of "hyssop," this manuscript has "hyssos." Hyssos was the Greek word for the short javelin which was carried by Roman soldiers. The picture then is placing the sponge upon the end of a javelin, and then lifting it up by the shaft to the lips of Jesus. The change represents a single letter, and it obtains a suitable meaning in this context. It can be harmonized easily with Matthew and Mark, for it simply specifies exactly what kind of a stick was used. This solution is so attractive that many have found it irresistible. There are two major objections, however, which render it extremely unlikely. (1) It is improbable that a generally inferior manuscript would be the only one in the entire manuscript tradition to preserve the correct reading at this point. (2) It is suspiciously easy to see why the hyssop would be changed into the javelin, but it is impossible to understand why the javelin would be changed into the hyssop, thus creating a problem for interpretation. It is always possible, of course, that "hyssop" represents a scribal error, but then the true text would expect to have been preserved in at least some other manuscript. It is clear that the hyssop is what John wrote.

A third effort to solve the problem is the identification of the hyssop with the caper plant, which has a stalk three or four feet high, and therefore can be visualized more easily in this role. This does not fit well with other occurrences of the word in the Bible, however, and this forces the additional hypothesis that different varieties or species are indicated in the different biblical texts.

A fourth effort at interpretation assumes that the

sponge was surrounded with the hyssop leaves and then both were placed upon the unmentioned javelin or perhaps simply on a reed or rod or stick. The point of the hyssop would then be the cooling effect provided by its leaves to the wine-soaked sponge. This would give a greater relief to the sufferer. This hypothesis assumes a greater concern in preparation for this act of kindness than would likely be found in reality. It is without any parallel in biblical usage.

Most likely is the association of the hyssop with the Old Testament sacrificial system its real meaning here. Of the twelve occurrences of the word in the Bible, if this text be excluded for the moment, only the reference to size in 1 Kings 4:33 is outside of a sacrificial or a cultic context. In Leviticus 14, the hyssop is part of the cultic process for cleansing from leprosy. In Numbers 19, it is associated with the sacrifice of the red heifer. In Psalms 51:7, the hyssop is used symbolically of cleansing in prayer. Hebrews 9:19 says that Moses sprinkled the people with hyssop after reading the Old Covenant at Mt. Sinai. The hyssop is a persistent part of the Old Testament theology of forgiveness and redemption. The story of the sprinkling of the door posts with blood at the first Passover (Exodus 12:22) especially established the use of hyssop within a sacrificial context. The mention of the hyssop during the Passover season would inevitably trigger many theological associations. For the Christian, the hyssop would inevitably suggest the Lamb of God, whose death upon the cross provided the relationship with God suggested by the Passover Lamb.

Since an average man could virtually reach the sponge to the lips of a man on a cross, even the small hyssop could easily give the extra few inches required for the action envisioned here. The symbolism of the hyssop in sacrifice is the probable explanation for the specification of the hyssop here instead of a stick. It is inexplicable that pagan Roman soldiers would have brought the hyssop for this purpose, however, and this forces the final question. Was there any real hyssop involved on a biological level? Or did not the soldiers use the stick which is mentioned in Matthew and Mark? And then did not John insert the hyssop in a profound theological symbolism, which is more "real" in ultimate terms than a minor detail regarding the exact nature of the stick used?

The Sixth Word

John 19:30

Verse 30. *Jesus drank the wine and said, "It is finished!" Then he bowed his head and died.*

"Jesus drank the wine." The greek verb can mean "took" (Phillips and NAB) or "received" (KJV, RSV, and NEB) but not really "drank" (TEV). The picture is of Jesus biting the sponge and then sucking in whatever drops of moisture he could. "Drink" in English does not adequately convey the idea. Jesus had refused the previous offer of a drugged drink to ease the pain of crucifixion (Matthew 27:34 and Mark 15:23). If we may interpret that refusal as a deliberate decision to face the experience of death in full possession of all of his mental powers, the voluntary nature of the death is again highlighted. Death is now so near that it can no longer be avoided. Jesus took the liquid refreshment, but this is not a drug and therefore has no narcotic effect. It is possible that Jesus took the wine to moisten his parched throat in order to be able to speak more easily the final shouted Words from the Cross. This is a popular interpretation of the scene. It is more probable, however, that Jesus accepted this drink for precisely the same reason he had refused the previous one. This slight refreshment would restore his vitality for the moment, so that he would be more fully conscious at the moment of death. The drink would retard the normal natural anesthetic which usually immediately precedes death.

This again highlights the voluntary nature of the death. The ultimate cause of the drink, however, was the fulfillment of prophecy. Steeped as he was in the Old Testament and conscious of the necessity of these things all taking place, it is possible that even the thirst appeared as part of the eternal plan expressed in prophecy.

". . . *and said, 'It is finished!'* " This is the same Greek verb which was used in verse 28 of the fulfillment or the "finishing" of Scripture. It is also identical in grammatical form. The progression of thought, apparently, is the recognition by Jesus in verse 28 that all has been finished, and that inner recognition is followed now by the spoken affirmation. It does not seem likely that a meaningful distinction can be made in the two occurrences of the verb, even though some have suggested that verse 28 involves the finishing of Scripture, and this verse involves the completion of the total work of redemption. Since it is all in Scripture, in John's view, to finish the Scripture is to do it all. The eternal plan of salvation has now been accomplished, and the human Jesus has no more to do. From the view-point of the eternal counsel of God, this is now the completion of the eternal possibilities for life available to men and women through their faith, and it has been done through the overcoming of the power of evil. From the post-resurrection view-point of the Christian, as well as in the eye of God, this is the decisive triumph of the power of God over the power of evil. Only to the eye of the non-believer can this death appear to be a defeat. The key, of course, to the affirmation of the completion of the plan of God at this point is that the resurrection to come is included in the "it is finished." The significance of this Word from the Cross, therefore, is that the last temptation has passed, and the irreversibility of the voluntary sacrifice of the Son of God has now been established. Until this point there had always been the dreadful "impossible possibility" that Jesus might yet decide not to drink the cup which had been prepared for him. Now the cup has been drained to the last drop, and salvation has essentially been accomplished for sinful men and women.

"Then he bowed his head." Death in crucifixion was actually caused by suffocation. Because of the way in which a person was placed upon the cross, it was possible to push upward with the feet in order to keep the chest cavity in a sufficiently upright position to allow breathing. As the body became too weak to continue this pressure, there was a collapse upon the cross, and the body hung as dead weight. When this happened the head dropped forward, the chest collapsed, breathing stopped, and death came from the resulting suffocation. The variation in the time it took to cause death is due to the variation in physical strength, or the will to live in the condemned.

The detail that Jesus' head dropped forward is found only in John. It is possible that John means simply to indicate by this detail the normal death of a person upon a cross, the head dropping forward upon the chest indicating the weakness of the body and the inability or unwillingness any longer to attempt to stand on tortured feet and legs. This is the interpretation implied in Phillips' translation, "his head fell forward." The verb was used in this sense, to indicate a weakness which caused a falling forward which in turn caused a disaster. A papyrus from the third century B.C. describes the sinking of a ship in this manner: "it came about that the right side of the ship listed (or dropped forward), and the ship thereby sank." The verb can also mean "to decline or to be far spent," and the cognate noun can be a bed upon which people sleep, continuing the association with the weakness of the body which forces sleep. It has been objected that this interpretation militates against the voluntary nature of the death, and especially the following phrase, "he handed over his spirit." This objection has little force, however, when it is considered that the voluntary nature of the death is established in the entire Passion narrative, including the trial, and not by any single detail. Jesus voluntarily put himself in the position where at last the weakness of the flesh would induce the normal death to be expected from a cross. This interpretation also takes seriously the fullness of the Incarnation and the reality of the death.

It is also possible, however, that Jesus deliberately bowed his head to induce the suffocation, thereby self-consciously selecting the moment of death. This interpretation stresses the voluntary nature of the death, and highlights Jesus as the active agent throughout. This is the apparent interpretation of the translations which use the active verb, "he bowed his head." The verb can be used actively of bowing or bending or inclining. There is a serious theological problem with this interpretation, for the plain implication is that Jesus deliberately cut short the process of the suffering at some point prior to what it would otherwise have been. This would be, in essence, an agreement to drink part of the cup prepared by the Father, but a refusal to drink all of it. In this sense, it is at least a partial degradation of the value of the death, and lessens the concept of the full obedience which Jesus claimed to have given the Father. This interpretation preserves the stress on the voluntary nature of the death (which is not needed when the total context is considered), at the expense of the completeness of the suffering.

It is more probable that Jesus did not cut short the suffering in any way. The weakness of the body caused the head to fall forward and thereby induced the death. This does not prevent additional symbolic layers of meaning from being seen in this particular choice of words. Aside from this verse, the phrase "to bow the head" is found only twice in the New Testament, and both times in the context of the Son of Man as having no place to lay his head upon earth. The reference is to a person's ability to lay down his own head in sleep upon his own pillow in his own bed in his own home (Matthew 8:20 and Luke 9:58). It is almost inevitable to note that at last the Son of Man did in fact find a place in which to lay down his head, even though his very own cross turned out to be his pillow. An amulet made for a Christian in the sixth century uses the word in a context of prayer, "I pray and bow my head." This idea of bowing the head in prayer, even though it represents a later usage, could yet fit in with the next phrase, to indicate a prayerful handing over of the spirit in death.

"... *and died.*" The Greek has "He handed over his spirit." This is most closely preserved in, "delivered over his spirit" (NAB) and "gave up his spirit" (KJV, RSV, and NEB). It is not a common phrase for death. Both Phillips and TEV have apparently thought that the form of the phrase has no significance, since they have both translated simply "and died." The ordinary meaning of the verb is to hand over some one or something to some one or to some other thing. There is a great deal of "handing over" in the Passion narrative. Judas handed over Jesus in the betrayal (Mark 14:10), the Sanhedrin handed over Jesus to Pilate (Mark 15:1), Pilate handed Jesus over to the will of the crowd (Luke 23:25), and then to the soldiers for execution (Mark 15:15). Jesus now hands over his life to the Father.

There are a number of specific ways in which the verb is used, and perhaps each contributes a layer of meaning to the total interpretation. (1) The handing over can be for the purpose of accountability. A lease for an oil-press in the second century A.D. contains the following clause: "at the end of the time I will deliver up the oil-press uninjured together with the doors and the keys belonging to it." Perhaps there is a hint that Jesus handed over his life to the Father for an accounting. The Incarnation is now complete, and the Father must now determine its acceptability. (2) The handing over may be for the purpose of judgment or punishment or even to serve a prison sentence. It is possible to connect this handing over with the Descent into Hell, consonant with one major interpretation of the cry of dereliction. (3) The handing over may be in confident trust and expectation that a good result will follow. A Christian letter from the third century speaks of the handing over of a woman into the care of good and faithful men until her son should arrive. In similar fashion, Jesus may be thought to hand over his life to the Father, trusting that good will somehow come of it. (4) The handing over may be completely voluntary and within his control. In this connection, John 10:18 should be noted: "I have the power to lay it (my life) down, and I have the power to take it up." The verb in our text may even be a self-conscious echo of this. (5) Handing over came to be a technical term for death, and in a second century work was used of the death of John. In Galatians 2:20, Paul used this verb of Christ's "handing himself over" for me. In Isaiah 53:12, the Septuagint used this verb, "handing over," but added "to death" in order to make the connection certain. Bernard believed that this verse represents a deliberate echo of the Hebrew text of Isaiah 53:12. The Suffering Servant "poured out his soul to death." The Septuagint turned this into the passive: "his soul was handed over to death." Now if John had used the same Greek verb as used in the Septuagint, but translated directly from the Hebrew, he would have just about the Greek text of this verse. The only difference is that John uses "spirit" (pneuma), while the Septuagint used "soul" (psyche). Nothing much can be made of this difference, however, because often the terms were used interchangeably, and because the phrase with "spirit" came to be used of death in martyrdom accounts.[1]

[1] J. H. Bernard, *A Critical and Exegetical Commentary on the Gospel According to St. John*, A. H. McNeile (ed), The International Critical Commentary (Edinburgh: T. and T. Clark, 1928), II:641.

The Seventh Word

Luke 23:44-49

Verse 44. *It was about twelve o'clock when the sun stopped shining and darkness covered the whole country until three o'clock;*

Verse 45. *. . . and the curtain hanging in the Temple was torn in two.*

"*. . . and the curtain hanging in the Temple.*" The Greek has simply "the veil" (or curtain) of the "sanctuary" (or temple). The first curtain separated the outer court from the Holy Place (Exodus 27:16). The second curtain separated the Holy Place from the Holy of Holies (Exodus 26:33; compare also Hebrews 9:3). The second curtain was made of fine twisted linen, with blue, purple, and scarlet hues. The design was made up of the Cherubim (Exodus 26:31). The curtain was fastened to two pillars. The only light to penetrate the Holy of Holies was that which could filter through the veil. Certain craftsmen were assigned the task of making and replacing the temple curtains on a regular basis, but it is not known how often this particular veil was replaced and under what conditions. The purpose of the second veil was to symbolize the separateness and remoteness of God. Access was denied to all laity, and only priests selected by lot twice daily and the high priest on the Day of Atonement were allowed to enter. Jewish tradition, not confirmed in the Old Testament, affirms that at this time there were two curtains, a cubit apart, which separated the Holy Place from the Holy of Holies. Whether one or two, the phrase "the veil of the temple" refers to the second of the two dividing curtains.

". . . *was torn in two.*" In our text this happened before the actual death, but when it was irreversibly imminent. Matthew 27:51 and Mark 15:38 have the rending of the veil take place after the death. They have the additional detail that it was torn "from top to bottom." The entire incident is omitted by John. It is no doubt significant that the tear was from top to bottom, as if God himself ripped the curtain in two. This exposed the Holy of Holies to common view and removed the remoteness and separateness. In this scene is symbolized the end of the Old Covenant and the beginning of the New Covenant. Aside from these references in the gospels, the "veil of the temple" occurs only in Hebrews in the New Testament. In 9:3 the curtain is identified as concealing the Holy of Holies. In 9:8, the purpose of the curtain is described as blocking the way into the sanctuary, or the presence of God. In 10:20, the curtain is identified symbolically as the flesh of Jesus. By his blood, Jesus opened the separating curtain so that Christians now have confidence to enter the sanctuary (10:19).

The symbolism is clear and perfect. The objective reality of the event has been questioned. Certainty is not possible, but if the curtain was actually torn — not only symbolically, the fact would be known to at least some of the priests. This could have had a bearing upon the many priests who became Christians (Acts 6:7). An early Christian tradition accounted for the tearing of the veil on the basis that the earthquake cracked one of the pillars to which the veil was fastened. Plummer cited a Jewish tradition that, forty years before the destruction of Jerusalem, the heavy gates of the temple, which could only with difficulty be moved by many men, flew open about midnight on the Passover. Josephus also reports an occurrence like this shortly before the capture of the city. "As Neander remarks, these accounts hint at *some strange occurrence* as being remembered in connexion with the time of the Crucifixion."[1] Only the postresurrection Christian faith, of course, could interpret the event as the significant symbol of the possibility of direct access to God in Jesus Christ.

> Verse 46. *Jesus cried out in a loud voice, "Father! In your hands I place my spirit!" He said this and died.*

"Jesus cried out in a loud voice." Matthew and Luke record the loud shout in connection with the cry of dereliction, while John omits it entirely. John has the bowing of the head and not the loud cry, while the other three Gospels have the loud shout and not the bowing of the head. Stephen also died with a loud shout (Acts 7:60), but stoning is not comparable as a cause of death. It is idle to speculate about a cause of death other than that normally caused by crucifixion. The voluntary nature of the death is established by the entire context, and not by any details such as this. Luke's language cannot readily be reproduced in English: "he phoned a great phone."

"Father!" The basic importance of the father-child relationship is expressed in the word itself. Our English word "father" comes from the German but is exactly the same word as the Greek *(pater)* and the Latin. The apparent difference is the spelling convention within the Indo-European Language Family known as Grimm's Law. There are two basic theories regarding its

[1] Alfred Plummer, *A Critical and Exegetical Commentary on the Gospel According to S. Luke.* The International Critical Commentary. 5th Edition. (Edinburgh: T. and T. Clark, 1922), p. 538.

etymology: (1) it may be from the root which means the protector or the nourisher; or (2) it may be childish babbling in imitation of the parents' speech, such as "daddy" and "poppa" in various languages. The Hebrew word *(ab)* is from a Semitic root which also has two possible etymological explanations: (1) it may be the one who decides, in allusion to patriarchal authority; or (2) it may be the childish babbling. Its Aramaic form *(abba)* has come into the New Testament. In the prayer at Gethsemane, the combination of the Aramaic and the Greek is seen in *"abba Pater"* (Mark 14:36).

The parent-child relationship is so important to human life that it was an obvious simile for the God-creature relationship. In the Old Testament, "Father" is found in connection with God as Creator (as in Deuteronomy 32:6 and Isaiah 64:8). God is seen as the Father also of the chosen people of Israel: "I am a Father to Israel and Ephraim is my first born" (Jeremiah 31:9). God has the persistent love of a Father even when the children are not worthy: "For You are our Father, though Israel does not acknowledge us . . . Redeemer is Your name from of old" (Isaiah 63:16). Especially relevant for the interpretation of this text, however, is the wistful expression in Jeremiah 3:19: "I thought you would call me 'My Father' and would not turn from following me."

Even though the Old Testament prepared the way for the concept of God as Father, there is an essential difference in the way it appeared on the lips of Jesus. In the Old Testament, the Father is essentially distant and is related more to Israel as a corporate entity than to individuals. The idea of "Father" is therefore more formal and symbolic than individual and real. Jesus saw the Father with the warmth and personal trust that the child in the nursery sees his or her own father. This application of family intimacy to God was essentially new. Jesus used the term "Father" as a personal address to God nineteen times in the four Gospels, in four different settings. He addressed the Father in thanksgiving (Matthew 11:25 and John 11:41), in the high priestly prayer (John 17:1), in the prayer at Gethsemane, and in connection with the cross.

"In your hands I place my spirit." It is possible that Psalms 31:5 came to Jesus' mind at this time. "Into thy hands I commit my spirit; thou hast redeemed me, O Lord, faithful God." Translations of the verb vary between "commend my spirit" (KJV, Phillips, and NAB), "commit" (RSV and NEB), and "place" (TEV). The basic meaning of the verb is "to hand over to another." Often, it is food which is placed before another or handed over. Jesus' parables and teachings were "handed over" to the people. A person can be committed or entrusted to the care and protection of another. In the papyri, it is found in the context of a letter of recommendation. Paul and Barnabas ordained elders for the churches and then "handed them over to the Lord" (Acts 14:23). Paul handed over to the Lord the elders of Ephesus (Acts 20:32). In the midst of persecution, Christians are to "hand over their souls to a faithful Creator" (1 Peter 4:19). This is an act of complete trust in God at the end.

"He said this and died." The verb translated as "died" is very unusual. It occurs only three times in the New Testament, and only in connection with the death of Jesus (Mark 15:37 and 39). Often, it is translated simply as "died" (Phillips, TEV, and NEB) or "expired" (NAB). The verb is cognate with "spirit," however, and some translations attempt to express this: "gave up the ghost" (KJV) and "breathed his last" (RSV). The word for "spirit" *(pneuma)* is related to the verb which means "to blow" and originally meant an elemental force which acts as a stream of moving air both in the natural wind and in the animal breath. Since the wind can be seen only in its effects of movement, there is an idea of mysterious energy inherent in the word. The mysterious

energy of the wind provided an obvious comparison with the Spirit of God (John 3:8). Since animal breath can be seen only in the movement caused by inhaling and exhaling, it was an obvious symbol for the life principle itself in contrast with the essential "lifelessness" of the flesh. It is this life principle which Jesus entrusted to the Father. He died when he breathed out or "blew out" the last of the life, leaving on the cross only a lifeless body. In Matthew 27:50, the death is described as "the spirit departed." In John 19:30, the phrase is "he handed over his spirit." It may be that the gospel writers are suggesting that there is something special about this death by their use of such unusual phrases.

Verse 47. *The army officer saw what had happened, and he praised God, saying, "Certainly he was a good man!"*

"The army officer saw what had happened." The Roman legion was divided into six cohorts of 1,000 men each. Each cohort was divided into ten "centuries" of 100 men each. Each century was commanded by a centurion (the army officer of TEV). It is difficult to give the equivalents in the current American military structure. It is clear that a legion would correspond to a division in the sense that it was the largest self-contained fighting unit which was standard throughout the army. The cohort is roughly the equivalent of a battalion and a century of a company. The problem with this identification is that the Romans did not have any headquarters which would correspond to the brigade. Considering the size of the modern American infantry division, which is three times the size of a legion, the Roman legion would seem to be more like a brigade. Its capacity for independent action, however, would differ significantly from the average brigade in the average division. If the separate infantry brigade were standard

instead of unusual, there would be a closer correspondence.

The second problem in identification comes from the fact that the Roman army did not have as many separate grades or ranks for enlisted and officer personnel as does the American army. The legion would be commanded by a tribune. There were six tribunes in a legion, and they would be considered as field grade officers, anywhere from major to full colonel. Each took his turn at commanding the legion during the year, and so there was not the sharp gradation of rank that the American army has. The tribunes appear to be the only officers in the legion. In order to have a "general," several legions would have to be grouped into a field army. The legate would be the deputy to the general.

It is not clear whether the centurion would be considered as a commissioned officer in the sense in which the term is used in the American army. Today a commissioned officer begins as a junior lieutenant and can expect to be promoted step by step to senior rank. No legal limits are imposed upon the rank he or she can hope to achieve. This was apparently not true in the Roman army. At the senior level, military grades were largely determined by political influence or at least required being a member of the aristocracy. A tribune would not normally expect to be able to become a legate, although a legate might become a general if he so desired. A centurion could not hope to be promoted to the rank of tribune. In this sense, it would not be considered a commissioned rank.

The rank of centurion was all that an ordinary soldier could hope to achieve. In that sense, it would appear to be a closer equivalent to the senior non-commissioned officer in the American army. Since there would be no junior "company grade" commissioned officers, the first sergeant would run the century even more completely than he does today. The centurion usually came up from the ranks and could hope to become the senior centurion of the first cohort, which would make him the "command sergeant major." There was a greater distance between the centurion and the middle level "sergeant," however, than would be true today between the first sergeant and other sergeants. If the American warrant officer, therefore, was the normal command rank for the infantry company, rather than being largely restricted to technical specialties, there would be the closest "fit." The warrant officer often comes from the ranks and does not progress to regular commissioned ranks. He or she is considered to be an officer, but can never achieve senior rank, and is the "bridge" between the enlisted and officer ranks.

With far fewer officers and virtually no staff positions competing for authority and prestige, a Roman centurion was a far more important figure than any American officer of comparable responsibility. The centurion figures prominently in the New Testament. In Matthew 8:5-13, in connection with the healing of his servant, Jesus said of the centurion that he had not found such great faith in Israel. In Acts 10:22-48, the conversion of the centurion Cornelius is so important that Peter performs the baptism, and the Holy Spirit was poured out in a "Gentile Pentecost." In Acts 27:1, the centurion Julius is in charge of taking Paul to Rome to stand trial. An unnamed centurion is in charge of the squad assigned the task of performing the crucifixion. Legend has given him the name of Longinus or Petronius, has assumed that he became a Christian, and was later martyred for his faith. He has been a popular subject for fiction even in our own time.

"... and he praised God." There is some variation in translation: "he glorified God" (KJV and NAB), "he praised God" (RSV, NEB, and TEV), and "he exclaimed reverently" (Phillips). The Greek verb is cognate with the glory *(doxa)* which is a basic characteristic of God. To recognize this glory in some way is to glorify God. When God does the glorifying, the verb means to be transformed in the next life in glory. When God is object, the verb means to praise, honor, or magnify in recognition of the person or acts of God. This has been interpreted in two ways: (1) assuming that the centurion was a proselyte believer, he first praised God and then spoke the following words; or (2) more probably, the words which he spoke in themselves constituted the praise. This does not require any assumption about the centurion's faith. His words are then an involuntary recognition of the glory of God as seen in the circumstances surrounding this death, including Jesus' own demeanor and attitude. It is almost a fulfillment of Matthew 5:16, "Let your light so shine before men, that they may see your good works and give glory to your Father who is in heaven." To give glory to God was one possible response to seeing a miracle (Matthew 9:8). In 2 Corinthians 9:13, glorifying God is defined as recognition of the gospel in obedience and in ministry to others. In Galatians 1:24, the conversion of Paul is made a reason for glorifying God. Here, the recognition that there is more in Jesus than a common criminal type, and that there is more in this death than an ordinary execution, is some recognition of the glory of God, whether intended consciously as such or not. Matthew and Mark do not say that the words of the centurion praised God, and John omits the incident entirely. In Mark 15:39, the words of the centurion are triggered by the sight of the death. In Matthew 27:54, they follow the earthquake and the exposure of the graves of the righteous.

"... *saying, 'Certainly he was a good man!'* " The translations reveal the difficulty in finding a single exact English equivalent: a "righteous" man (KJV), an "innocent" man (RSV, NEB, and NAB), and a "good" man (Phillips and TEV). The Greek word *(dikaios)* is often translated as "justify" when it is a verb and as "righteousness" or "justification" when it is a noun. It probably does not have a deep theological meaning in this particular text. In the papyri, the word is often used in the sense of "fair" or "just." The most basic idea in the word is upright or just, in the sense of a person who lives in accordance with the laws of God and man. Pilate's wife used this adjective to describe Jesus in Matthew 27:19, and Pilate himself used it of Jesus in Matthew 27:24, in his disclaimer of guilt in Jesus. These instances have led some to conclude that "innocent" is the basic meaning on the lips of the centurion as well. Mere innocence, however, would most likely not have produced such an impression. A glimpse of "goodness" in Jesus which went far beyond the mere fact of innocence accounts better for the feelings of Pilate's wife and the centurion. In Matthew 27:54 and Mark 15:39, the centurion says that Jesus is the Son of God. In this text in Luke, it sounds more as if he saw something that touched his battle-hardened sensibilities in a way he did not fully understand, than that he made a full confession of faith in Jesus as the Messiah. In Matthew, it sounds more like a confession of faith. In any case, the tradition is firm that the centurion was touched and was moved to make a response.

Verse 48. *When the people who had gathered there to watch the spectacle saw what happened, they all went back home, beating their breasts in sorrow.*

"*. . . when the people who had gathered there to watch the spectacle saw what happened.*" This is the "neutral" part of the crowd who watched the crucifixion. These people are not favorably disposed towards Jesus, as are his followers, but they are not actively opposed to him either, as are the priestly and Pharisaic classes. These are the average light-hearted people who went out to watch the "show" in the same spirit in which we might go to a ball game or to the theatre. The Greek word behind the translations "sight" (KJV and RSV) and "spectacle" (Phillips, NEB, NAB, and TEV) occurs only here in the New Testament. In 3 Maccabees 5:24, it is used of "a piteous spectacle" which the crowds had assembled to watch. A pagan Egyptian king had decided to eliminate the Jews, and they were to be trampled to death by drunken elephants. The crowd came to root for the elephants.

"... *they all went back home, beating their breasts in sorrow.*" In some strange way, the "show" had not proven to be the light entertainment they had expected. Disturbed and upset by the experience, they returned to their homes thoughtfully and in some sort of a mood of sorrowful regret for what they had seen. Perhaps this can be connected, in tone at least, with Jesus' words to the daughters of Jerusalem when he was on the way to the cross (Luke 23:28-31). There the reference seems to be to the approaching judgment of God which will result in the destruction of Jerusalem. The apocryphal *Gospel of Peter* has apparently made this connection: they "returned, saying, 'Alas, what things have been done to us by our sins; for the destruction of Jerusalem has approached' " (Gospel of Peter 7:25). The Old Syriac inserts at this point: "Woe to us! What has befallen us? Woe to us from our sins!" Perhaps there is a reference to Zechariah 12:10: "when they look upon him whom they have pierced, they shall mourn for him, as one mourns for an only child, and weep bitterly over him, as one weeps over a first-born." It is not likely that Zechariah has in mind the death of the Messiah; the people have martyred some one and he tells them that they will bitterly regret having done it. Here some of the people have apparently begun already to wonder if they have witnessed a good thing or not.

Verse 49. All those who knew Jesus personally, including the women who had followed him from Galilee, stood at a distance to watch.

There is a painful contrast between the crowd leaving the scene and the small faithful remnant who remained to the bitter end. The crowd had come for a spectacle, but these had watched with far different emotions, and therefore a more normal word for "seeing" is used. In Matthew 27:55 and Mark 15:40-41, only women are mentioned, but this text includes men and women. "Those who knew" is masculine and therefore includes the entire group who remained to the end, men and women alike. The women are mentioned because their display of faithfulness would be unusual. The verbal form for "to watch" is feminine. This has led some to infer that the men stood farther back, out of fear, while the braver women came closer to the cross. This is so improbable as to be ludicrous. The verbal form is feminine because "women" is the closer antecedent in the sentence. All accounts agree that they stood afar off because it would be imprudent to come close. Aside from John and the women who are named, it is impossible to identify them. From their boldness in claiming the body, it is possible that Nicodemus and Joseph of Arimathea were among the sympathetic watchers at the end.

The Cosmic Signs

Matthew 27:51-54

Verse 51. *Then the curtain hanging in the Temple was torn in two from top to bottom. The earth shook, the rocks split apart,*

Palestine seems to have averaged slightly more than one major destructive earthquake per century and between two and six light shocks per year. It is not improbable, therefore, that an earthquake of light proportions actually happened at this time. The rending of the veil is often considered as having been caused by the shock. Josephus records that the priests felt a quaking at a Pentecost feast preceding the fall of Jerusalem. The Talmud records the opening of the doors of the Temple. "A cleavage in the masonry of the porch, which rent the outer veil and left the Holy Place open to view, would account for the language of the gospels, of Josephus, and of the Talmud."[1] The tremor could not have been severe enough to topple the crosses at Golgotha however, or to frighten the crowds. The centurion, it should be noted, remained at his post at the cross. There may have been a light shock at the Temple area which did not extend very far.

In any case, it is the symbolic value of the earthquake

---

[1]Willoughby C. Allen, *A Critical and Exegetical Commentary on the Gospel According to S. Matthew.* The International Critical Commentary. Third Edition (Edinburgh: T. and T. Clark, 1912), p. 296.

which is important. The same verb is used for the splitting open of the rocks and for the splitting of the veil. In the Old Testament, earthquakes are associated with the presence of God (Exodus 19:18, Judges 5:5, and Psalms 68:8) as well as with the anger of God (2 Samuel 22:8 and Isaiah 29:6). When Elijah hid in the desert a whirlwind split the rocks and an earthquake came, but God was in neither (1 Kings 19:11). In Matthew 24:7, earthquakes are a sign of the beginning of the end of the world, and in Revelation 6:12 an earthquake follows the opening of the Sixth Seal. The cosmic signs have a cumulative effect. If the earthquake is causally connected with the rending of the veil of the Temple, and if the earthquake is a sign of the end of the world in the judgment of God, then the death of Jesus is set in eternal terms. It is a sign that the old order of the world, which includes the Temple, has been rendered obsolete in this death, and that a new order of being commences. The significance of the earthquake, however, like the darkness, is apparent only to the eye of faith after the fact and in the light of the resurrection.

Verse 52. *the graves broke open, and many of God's people who had died were raised to life.*

Verse 53. *They left the graves, and after Jesus rose from death, they went into the Holy City, where many people saw them.*

". . . *the graves broke open.*" The shock of the earthquake, which split the rocks, broke open the graves around Jerusalem and exposed the bodies to view. As the text now stands, this happened at the time of the death, before the thrusting of the spear into the side of Jesus. This means that it was still some hours before the beginning of the Sabbath. The shock of the earthquake may have damaged the porch of the Temple, and it must have extended beyond the city limits in order to break open the tombs. There is no evidence, however, that it extended to Golgotha; for a shock strong enough to break open the tombs like this would have toppled the crosses. The centurion shows awareness of the earthquake, but he remains at his post. There is no evidence that anyone else was aware of the earthquake. There is no terror or panic in the watching crowd.·

"... and many of God's people who had died." These are the "saints" (KJV, RSV, and NAB) or the "holy men" (Phillips) or "God's people" (NEB and TEV). This is the only occurrence of "the saints" (oi agioi) in the gospels. Elsewhere it is used in the New Testament only of Christians. Two interpretations are possible: (1) they are the people who have acknowledged Jesus as the Messiah and then died before the crucifixion, such as Simeon and Anna. The advantage of this interpretation is that it preserves consistency in the New Testament usage of "saints." It is doubtful, however, that there would be "many" in this category. Their resurrection as believers, moreover, would be a point almost too obvious for such a mighty "sign" as this. Or: (2) they are the holy men and women of Israel who lived and died before the incarnation, such as the patriarchs and prophets. There was a widespread belief that they would be resurrected as a prelude to the final consummation of all things. This is more likely, for it would fulfill Messianic expectation, and would also make the point that the benefits of the crucifixion extended backwards in time as well as forwards. Thus, it would make the same point as the Descent into Hell.

"... and after Jesus rose from death." The problem for exegesis is the sequence of events. If the graves broke open at the death, and if the saints did not go into Jerusalem until after the resurrection, we must consider their situation during this intervening time period. The bodies may be conceived as lying in their graves exposed to view during this time. It is possible that Sabbath rules would have prevented the covering of the bodies. The stark and somber sight of open graves would be an appropriate symbol of the time in which Jesus also lay in the grave. Until the resurrection of Jesus, such hopeless death would seem to be the only end of man.

It is also possible to read the text, however, that they were raised to life as soon as the graves were split open, and that they left their graves, but they did not appear in Jerusalem until after the resurrection. This is a more natural reading of the text. We cannot visualize the whereabouts of the resurrected saints during this time, however, for they have left their graves and are presumably "in hiding" until the proper time to make an appearance. The posing of such a question reveals the extreme difficulty of understanding this on a realistic level.

Theologically, the resurrection of the saints would fit better if it were placed immediately after the resurrection of Jesus. Then it would be the perfect symbol of the effect of that resurrection upon men and women. The phrase "after Jesus rose" does place it in that context. One solution to the difficulty begins with the fact that a second earthquake is associated with the resurrection of Jesus (Matthew 28:2). The tradition may have confused the two earthquakes and placed the breaking open of the graves with the wrong earthquake. This is very plausible and it makes excellent sense. The primary objection, however, is that there is simply no textual problem with these verses. If such a dislocation occurred, it took place before the earliest of our existing manuscripts. On the basis of a virtually unanimous textual tradition at this point, we can only assume that Matthew placed the account in connection with the death, where it now stands.

This leaves us with the theological problem that the resurrection of these saints is connected with the death of Jesus more than with the resurrection. A second solution to the problem has been to associate this with the Descent into Hell. This gives the same ambiguity to the dead bodies of the saints during the intervening time as exists with the body of Jesus during the same time. It accounts for the double connection with the death and the resurrection. It fits its immediate context, therefore, and does not require any assumptions as to the transmission of the tradition or the text. Theologically, it answers the question about the destiny of those who lived before the incarnation and ties all salvation firmly to the death and resurrection of Jesus Christ. It allows for the preaching to the spirits in hell to take place between the death and the resuurection. On a symbolic level, this interpretation presents no problems. On a realistic level, this requires the assumption that the dead bodies were exposed in their graves during this time and did not leave their graves in a resurrected state until after the resurrection of Jesus.

The third possibility involves assumptions concerning the transmission of the text or tradition in a different direction than the assumption of a dislocation. It is possible that the original tradition envisioned the resurrection of these saints as occurring immediately in connection with the death of Jesus and their appearance in Jerusalem at once. This would be a natural reading of the text in this location. The problem to a later editor would be the contradiction to 1 Corinthians 15:20, which affirms that Christ is the firstfruits of them that slept. To alleviate this difficulty, "after Jesus rose" was added as a parenthesis. The result was the difficulty in the sequence of events.

"... *were raised to life. They left the graves ... they went into the Holy City, where many people saw them.*" The text does not record the reaction of the people when they saw these resurrected ones walking the streets of Jerusalem. It is very strange that no reaction is recorded regarding such an unusual sight. We are assured that they were seen, and so the story is not told solely for its symbolic value. The lack of reaction is a striking confirmation of Luke 16:31: "If they do not hear Moses and the prophets, neither will they be convinced if some one should rise from the dead." The most reasonable explanation is that the "many" who saw them were Christians, and that therefore they were visible only to the eye of faith. The sight of the risen Christ had the ability to produce faith. It is less certain that the sight of these resurrected "saints" had an evangelistic effect. It is, of course, always a possibility that they were seen by those who were ready to become believers, and that the sight contributed to their conversion. To a modern reader, however, it does not matter. What does matter is the profound reality of the symbolism which included those before Christ as well as those after Christ in the grace offered by God through the crucifixion and resurrection of Jesus Christ.

Verse 54. *When the army officer and the soldiers with him, who were watching Jesus, saw the earthquake and everything else that happened, they were terrified and said, "He really was the Son of God!"*

Three interpretations have been given of the words spoken here at this time. (1) It may represent a full confession of faith in Jesus as the Messiah. Christian tradition, giving the name of Petronius as well as Longinus to the centurion, assumed that this involved his conversion and developed stories about his later conduct as a Christian. It is possible that a veteran Roman soldier had become a proselyte to Judasim and therefore was theologically prepared for this. We do read of other centurions who came to faith. It is also possible that he had not been a proselyte, but had heard enough through his service in Palestine to understand what the astounding events suggested to him. (2) It may represent simply an involuntary recognition that Jesus was a good man, closer to what Luke records. The difficulty with this is its incongruence with the terror. (3) It may represent a confession that Jesus was a "hero' in the sense of Greek mythology. The hero was a human being who had divine characteristics and eventually became a god. The unusual phenomena associated with the death may have suggested a Hercules-like figure to the pagan centurion. This accounts for the fear and also does not require the assumption of a confession of Christian faith. The decline of faith in pagan heroes in this period, however, must be taken into account. On balance, considering it as a genuine confession of faith seems the most reasonable interpretation.